Fonders End Library
College Court
High Street
Enfield
Tel. 443 2313

21. MAY
11. NOV
AUG
15. DEC
18. OCT
18. OCT
RZ 9/02

LONDON BOROUGH OF ENFIELD
LIBRARY SERVICES

This item should be RETURNED on or before the latest date stamped. You may obtain a renewal by personal call, telephone or post. You should quote the date due for return, the bar code number and your personal library number. Overdue items will incur charges.

30126 00806948 3

Sexual Assault: How to Defend Yourself

by
Dan Lena and Marie Howard

Library of Congress Cataloging-in Publication Data

Lena, Dan.

   Sexual assault: how to defend yourself

     1. Self-respect. 2. Assertiveness (Psychology)
I. Lena, Marie. II.Title.
BF697.5.S46L46 1987   158'.1   87-7522
ISBN 0-8119-0677-9

Copyright © 1990 by Dan Lena

All rights reserved. No part of this work may be reproduced or used in any form or by any means--graphic, electronic, or mechanical, including photocopying, recording,
taping or information storage and retrieval systems--without permission in writing from the publisher.

For information:

Fell Publishers, Inc.
2131 Hollywood Boulevard
Hollywood, FL 33020

People Against Rape
P.O. Box 160
Elmwood Park, IL 60635

Published simultaneously in Canada by
Prentice-Hall, Inc., Ontario, Canada

Manufactured in the United States of America
1234567890

iv

Comments

"Growing numbers of women and children are learning to prevent sexual assaults with assertiveness training and martial arts...On Friday in Chicago, People Against Rape will train 1,600 girls – the organization's biggest session ever..."
Sam Meddis
Cover Story, USA Today

"The couple [Lenas] also instruct students on positive thinking because they have found many high school students – male and female – already are guilt-ridden from an assault or attempted assault."
Tina Ross
News Sun Tattler
Hollywood, Florida

"More than 38,000 students will watch their Hands Off: I'm Special campaign this year. Their first Detroit-area lesson will begin with self-esteem...It's a far more eye-catching educational technique than a lecture delivered from a podium."
Neal Rubin
Detroit Free Press

"I have never seen such positive energy start so early in the show and so explosively and continue to the end. Marie and Dan played off each other quite well, and their spontaneous role-playing added greatly to the excitement."
John DeBerry
Religious Programming Coordinator
WBBM TV (CBS, Inc.), Chicago

"I think the 'Dynamic Duo' might be an appropriate name to describe you. The bottom line: you promote respect between men and women."
Maureen Bonner
Purdue University Women's Awareness Department

"It did not look like a seminar on rape...The performance was effective. The students responded to the humor and yet got the serious point. After 10 years of talking to kids about rape, the pair have their performance honed to a cadence that many a comedy team would envy."
Dave Vorga
The Eccentric
Birmingham, Michigan

Special Thanks to:

Paul Natkin
for self-defense and exercise photos.

Mary LaMonte
for cover photo.

Our wonderful parents
Sal Lena, Angie Lena, and Mary Howard
for bringing us up to understand that we are special
and our life has a purpose.
We love you.

Our dear friend and advisor,
William Phillips.

Monte, for "coming through" when we needed you.

Cliff, Lisa and the entire Lena family.

Two special children, Brandi and Daniel Joseph.
We love you.

Bill Ludewig and Sr. Helen.

Our students over the years who keep us "young."

And special appreciation to those individuals
who related their personal experiences
for use in this book.
Thank you for your contributions.

God bless all of you!

About the Authors

Dan Lena and Marie Howard are a husband and wife team who travel around the United States presenting their Hands Off: I'm Special workshops to students of all ages.

Dan and Marie formed People Against Rape in 1976 and since then have personally instructed over 250,000 students. Their commitment and drive stem from personal experiences—both were sexually attacked. Dan, at 11 years old, was assaulted, but managed to escape. Marie, at age 15, was beaten and raped in a hitchhiking incident. They met years later when Marie walked into Dan's karate studio to learn self-defense and karate.

Their common interest in self-defense expanded to police science and crisis intervention training. Their personal relationship also grew, and they were married in 1983.

Initially, they began teaching at one high school with a class of 30 girls. But they had a goal to teach all over the United States. Pooling their resources, they developed Hands Off: I'm Special from a philosophy into what it is today—a national campaign with three goals: to heighten awareness about the crime of rape, to develop self-esteem in all people, and to prevent sexual assaults. They now teach over 70,000 students a year—male and female.

Dan and Marie are an energetic, fun-loving couple who take life one day at a time. They are excellent role models for their students, and their outgoing and dynamic personalities make learning about self-defense and rape prevention a positive and fun experience.

Admittedly, their controversial programs are not without critics. Some people disapprove of Dan and Marie's often blunt approach to such an indelicate subject or their use of theatrics and improvisation to deliver their message. However, the couple feels that it is necessary to deal with this topic in as realistic and thought-provoking a manner as possible.

Dan and Marie are both karate black belts, competitive body-builders, and vegetarians. They are motivational consultants to athletic teams, health spas, universities, and corporations. They have co-authored My Power Book—a motivational workbook designed to help the reader rid himself of guilt in order to achieve personal success.

Dan and Marie's philosophy on life is evident in every facet of their teaching. Their belief that everyone is special and has a specific purpose is stressed constantly in their workshops. They will not be satisfied until there is a wave of self-confidence in this world so powerful that people will be able to rise above any problems put before them.

"God made you, and God doesn't make mistakes," says Marie.

"You are nature's greatest gift, and no one has the right to make you feel less than you are," adds Dan.

Contents

About the Authors . . . . *vii*
Introduction . . . . *xi*

Chapter 1   Rape...A Joke? 1

Chapter 2   Types of Rape 15

Chapter 3   Who Rapes...And Why 33

Chapter 4   Order in Which a Rape Occurs 37

Chapter 5   A Women's Options 41

Chapter 6   Self-Defense Techniques 49

Chapter 7   Conditioning Exercises 67

Chapter 8   Natural Defenses 81

Chapter 9   I Need Answers 85

Chapter 10 Personal Experiences 97

Chapter 11 Overcoming the Attack 119

Introduction...

This book was written by two people who believe wholeheartedly in the prevention of sexual assault and the preservation of personal rights. Consider this a self-help book designed to make you more knowledgeable about what rape is, how it happens, and how you can prevent it by using your natural defenses and actual self-defense techniques.

We will not tell you what you can't do — don't walk down dark alleys, don't go out at night alone, don't be too friendly. We will only suggest things that you can do. We will lean towards the positive on everything — even while discussing the violent crime of rape.

Thousands of women have been victimized by all types of rape, including not only the "classic" form, but also the "little rapes" — the visual and verbal attacks, the flashers, the obscene phone calls, and various other daily humiliations. We want to arm you with the tools to deal with these situations.

Our national campaign against sexual assault is called "Hands Off: I'm Special." But it is more than a name, it is an attitude. We want you to make these words a part of your life.

You have a purpose in your life — a reason for being. You have dreams, desires, and aspirations. You might not even know what your purpose is, but whatever it might be, you are too special and too important to take abuse from anyone. And we mean anyone! When someone tries to dish out some dirt to you, throw it back at them...Say "Hands Off: I'm Special!" Start believing that.

It may be difficult to imagine yourself as being special, but think about it this way: You might not be *Vogue's* or *Glamour's* idea of the "perfect" woman, but the very fact that you are different makes you unique. By being unique, you are rare. Through the centuries, people have valued and cherished rarity. So why should you not value and cherish yourself for being rare and different?

Most women are terrified with the thought of being raped. Overcome fear with knowledge. Replace submissiveness with assertiveness. Fight guilt with a positive mental attitude. Develop self-confidence. Be the person you want to be. Take control of your life, and join the living.

You are nature's greatest gift, so say...

HANDS OFF!

Sexual Assault: How to Defend Yourself

Chapter 1

Rape...A Joke?

Marie's story

    Sometimes I can remember everything about it. Other times, small details escape my memory. There are some parts that I'll never forget.
    I was 15 years old when it happened. I was hitch-hiking down the boulevard to go meet my boyfriend that early fall evening. I didn't hitch like everyone else, though. I was too smart for that. Instead of sticking my thumb out, I would wait for the cars to stop by the stoplight, and if I thought the guy inside looked "all right," I would tap on the window and ask him for a ride. To me, that method seemed less dangerous.
    I was in a hurry that evening because my boyfriend didn't like it when I was late, and I hadn't had any luck getting a ride. Finally, an old beat-up Chevy stopped by the light. I did look inside, but I couldn't see much because I wasn't wearing my glasses. I motioned to the driver, and he signaled for me to open the door and get in. I had no idea what a mistake that was going to be.
    Once inside, I got a better look at the driver and became slightly alarmed. I did my best to hide my apprehension. He was a Hispanic man in his mid-twenties, wearing a leather vest with chains on it. He was sporting large tattooed biceps. His head was bald, and he wore several silver rings on his fingers.

The car was filthy. There were broken bottles, empty cans, tools, and paper debris cluttering the floor of the car. The back window had been shattered and was covered with plastic. I tried not to look shocked, so I casually said hello and asked him how far he was going.

"I'll take you as far as you want to go, mama," he said, with a thick Spanish accent.

I told him where I was going, and we drove off.

I started to make small talk, trying to engage in "neutral" conversation, but he kept talking about my looks, or my boyfriends, or things I like to do for fun. I was leary, but I had been in this type of situation before, so I felt I could handle it. Besides, we were getting closer to my destination.

We came to a stoplight by Humboldt Park, a high-crime area in Chicago, noted for its racial rioting and gang warfare. The driver turned down Humboldt Drive which led into the park. Immediately, I questioned his move, as it was not necessary to turn.

He said, "Don't worry. I'm taking a different route." His voice took on a new tone now--more commanding, slightly agitated by my question.

I knew something was definitely wrong. He was circling the park, looking around nervously. It was really dark now, and it was difficult to see inside the park, but he seemed to know exactly where he was going. That frightened me. We came to a stoplight, and I thought about jumping out. My eyes peered down to the handle of the door, and fear overcame me as I saw there was no handle on the inside.

"How did he open the door for me?" I thought to myself. Then I remembered that he had motioned to me to open the door. "I opened it from the outside!"

"Okay, Marie, keep a cool head. You'll get out of this," I told myself.

I was silent; so was he. We were both sweating. I was sweating for a different reason than he was. My mouth was getting dry.

A Chicago police squad car pulled right up alongside of us.

"I have to get their attention!" I thought. "But what if they don't see me? What if they don't know what I'm trying to say?"

I looked over at my driver, and he smiled at me as if he knew what I was thinking. I turned back towards the squad car and watched it turn right, away from the park. My last hope for help was gone.

My driver breathed a sigh of relief.

"Please, I really have to get where I'm going. Take me there now," I insisted.

"Don't worry about it, baby. I'll take you where you're going. We're going to have some fun first."

With that, he turned onto a small road leading into the park.

I had to think fast. In a stern voice, I commanded, "Take me to Augusta Boulevard right now. I'm not fooling around!"

He slammed on the brakes hard and turned towards me with the most hateful look I have ever seen. With the back of his hand, he cracked me across the side of my face so hard that the door-mounted armrest I was clutching onto ripped off the side of the door. The force of the blow thrust my body towards him. I knew my face was swelling, as I literally saw stars when he hit me. I started crying uncontrollably.

That made him angry. He began repeating, "Shut up, bitch! Shut up! Shut up!"

"Please don't do this," I pleaded. "Don't hurt me."

He screamed at me, "All you bitches are alike. You treat men like shit; then you start crying, begging for our forgiveness. You're all alike, all you fuckin' bitches." He was breathing heavily, trying to catch his breath, as if he were overcome with emotion.

"I never did anything to you," I told him. "I wasn't a bitch to you."

I was trying to diffuse his anger, and he didn't like it. Without any warning, he reached over and grabbed a handful of my long, curly hair and yanked my head down so hard that my forehead hit the steering wheel. It's strange, but I can remember hearing my hair being ripped out of my head. The sound came from inside of my head, like when you're under water and you can hear your breathing and movement. It was a sound like that.

When I lifted my head, he was laughing. He was holding my hair in his hand, displaying it to me. "Nice hair," he said. "I think

I'll keep it for decoration." He gently laid it on top of the rearview mirror, like one would hang a baby shoe.

The park lamp provided a light that made my hair shine as it hung off the mirror and gently swayed with the breeze. It felt like the inside of my head had been ripped out with my hair. I felt my head swell up now. It was a throbbing pain.

I knew there was nothing I could do. For over an hour, he told me about how all of the women in his life had mistreated him. I just listened.

Then he stopped talking. He started the car and began driving. I assumed it was all over. I thought he was taking me to the nearest street to drop me off. Instead, he drove more deeply into the park where construction was underway to build a small lake for the local residents. There were tractors and earth-movers scattered all over. He drove up a small hill and parked. I looked out of my window, and there was nothing but a huge ditch that dropped down hundreds of feet.

"Oh my God!" I thought. "He's going to kill me and dump me in this ditch. No one will ever find me. My mother doesn't know where I am. No one does."

There was a sign explaining the construction, right next to where we were parked. I remember thinking how ironic it was that the sign read:

> **FUTURE SITE OF THE HUMBOLDT PARK LAKE.**
> **FUN, RELAXATION, AND RECREATION FOR ALL.**
> **COME SPEND A PLEASANT SUNDAY AFTERNOON.**

To me, this site was the place of my death.

I tried to separate myself from the entire situation. I mentally prepared for the worst. It's true that your life passes in front of you when you think you are going to die. I was staring into the front window of the car, and in the reflection, I saw myself as a child wearing this little Annie Oakley outfit that I used to have when I was about four years old. I saw it as clear as day. I had a little leather holster with two guns that I used to draw in mock gun battle. I thought back on times that I would otherwise never have remembered – times when I was two and three years old.

Then the scene in my mind changed. I saw my body lying in the ditch covered with dirt. I saw a big tractor digging the gound up and finding my body, naked. That scene brought me back to reality. My heart was racing, and I was having a hard time breathing.

The attacker reached down under his seat and pulled out a small mirror and a single-edged razor blade. He pulled a small plastic bag out of his vest pocket and opened it. He poured some powder on the mirror, looked down on the floor of the car, and ordered me to pick up a small straw that was lying amidst all the other garbage. I gave it to him, and after he used the razor blade to cut and smoothe out the white powder, he put the straw to his nose and snorted the substance.

"Hey, you didn't want any, did you, baby?" he asked as he threw the mirror, the razor blade, and the straw down on the floor by my feet.

My mind started racing when the razor blade bounced off a bottle and hit my foot. I thought about picking it up and using it on him so I could escape!

My thoughts were abruptly interrupted as he started telling me what he was going to do to me. He moved closer to me and put one arm around me and, with the other hand, began stroking my face where he had hit me. He told me that I was a "beautiful young thing" and bragged about how he "fucked" 15-year-old girls all the time. He told me how much they loved him and begged him for sex, "just like you're going to after I get done with you."

I was sobbing, desperately trying to hold back the tears, knowing that crying would only make him angry. He was talking filthy now, calling me names and degrading me. I was very humiliated that he was talking to me about disgusting sexual acts that he just assumed I knew about. I remember being mad about that, but I knew I couldn't say anything to him in response.

For some inexplicable reason, he turned away from me and peered outside. Maybe he thought he heard a noise; maybe he was getting high and paranoid. As he was looking around, I quickly bent over and picked up the razor blade, squeezing it tightly in my right hand. I had to hide it.

He brought his attention back to me now and started to unbuckle my pants. He reached down inside my blouse and ripped my bra off. He did many things to me, and then he raped me.

The whole time, I clutched the razor blade in my hand. I wanted to use it so badly, but I decided against doing so. I imagined his taking it away from me and using it on me to slash my face and eventually kill me. I was holding onto it so tightly now that I felt it digging into me, slicing my thumb. I still have that scar to remind me of the experience.

He was lying on top of me as I was propped up slightly against the door. My mouth was so dry that I could hardly open it. My adrenaline was so high that I could feel the blood racing through my veins. I can't remember everything that happened in the short amount of time that followed, but I do remember getting very angry that he was biting my chest and breasts, tearing my skin with his teeth.

I realized I had to take a chance. "It's him or me, and it can't be me. I've got to get out of here alive."

His head was down. He wasn't even paying attention to me. It was as if I wasn't even a person--he was just doing whatever he wanted to with my body. That made me so angry. I had to get angry to do what I was about to do.

I brought my arm around and held my hand up. He looked up slightly as if he were mad about the slight disturbance. As his eyes met mine, I plunged the razor blade into his forehead, and with a powerful swipe, slashed his entire face diagonally. I cut across his eye, and for a brief moment, I was repulsed as I felt the bump in his nose, but I proceeded past it anyway, across his lips and chin. Blood gushed out, and I quickly dropped the blade.

He immediately brought his hands up to cover his face, and so clearly--like it happened yesterday--I can remember the blood pouring out through his fingers. He screamed in agony, like he was dying. I pushed him off of me and had to crawl over him to get out of the car from his side. As he groped for me with one hand, I knocked his hand off of me.

I opened up his door and fell out of the car. I quickly got to my feet and pulled my pants up. I had to run through Humboldt Park to get back to the main street. I ran frantically, hearing his blood-curdling scream. I'll never forget that sound. In fact, I heard it over and over again in the nightmares that followed for months later.

Despite the difficulty of running in my giant bell-bottom pants, I made it to the main street, about a mile away, in what seemed to be all of two minutes.

Out of breath, I began walking down the boulevard. I decided to meet my boyfriend, thinking that I would get some help from him. Besides, our meeting point was closer than my home. As I was walking, I saw a police car. I flagged it down.

The police officers saw my condition--my face and eyes were black and blue, my hair was all over the place, there was blood on my clothes, and my face was soaked with tears and blood. They jumped out of the car and came to my aid.

When they asked me what had happened, I told them I was assaulted and raped. They put me in the back of the car and headed towards the nearest hospital. They began to fill out the police report and then inquired as to how I was placed at the scene.

"How did he get you into the car?" asked the officer.

"I was hitchhiking," I replied.

With that, the driver stopped the car, and the officer filling out the report dropped the clipboard, got out of the car, opened up my door, and said, "Get out, you little bitch."

Shocked, I asked him why.

"Only whores hitchhike. You deserve what happened to you. You're lucky we don't arrest you for hitchhiking. Now get out."

In disbelief, I left and walked to the place where my boyfriend and I had agreed to meet. He was in a car kissing another girl. I tapped on the window, and he angrily got out.

"What happened to you?" he demanded. "You're late!"

I told him what had happened. He slapped me across the face and said, "I told you never to get into a car with a different guy. You probably wanted it, didn't you?"

Devastated, I walked home.

By the time I got there, it was almost midnight. My mother asked what happened to me. I couldn't tell her I was hitchhiking because she had told me never to hitchhike. I couldn't tell her where I had been going because I wasn't allowed to date that guy, and I had been sneaking to meet him. Besides, I thought she would blame me for the rape the way the others had. So I told her that I got into a gang fight with some girls in the neighborhood. I was grounded for fighting.

I never reported it. I never got counseling.

Dan's story

It happened on Halloween night; I was ll years old. At about 4:00 in the afternoon, my mother and sister started to get us all ready for the fun evening ahead. Both of my younger brothers wore the "traditional" Halloween costumes. But for me, the decision this year was to dress up as a girl. My mother and sister had great plans for me--a red blouse, dark skirt, navy pumps, earrings, and, of course, plenty of makeup.

Everything was going fine until I walked out of the door of our suburban home. As I left to meet my friends, a car drove past, and two guys yelled out, "Hey baby! How about a trick or a few of our treats?!"

It only took me about five minutes of being "female" to realize how many humiliations women have to endure--the stares from strangers, the verbal put-downs, the abusive language, etc.

At about 5:30, I met up with my friends at the corner store, but I didn't get the usual reception. They all backed away; two of them laughed and called me a "fag."

One said, "What the hell are you doing? You can't go out with us looking like a *girl*. What would everyone think?"

"They would think it was Halloween, and I was dressed like a girl," I replied sarcastically. "Besides, what's the difference what anyone else thinks, anyway?"

One of them insisted, "No way we're going around with a fag." The others agreed, and soon I was alone.

By the time I began trick-or-treating, the streets were full of moms and dads accompanying their young children, and the older kids were making mischief as usual. Before this night, my memories of Halloween had been pleasant ones. But now I was finding out about a different side of life. As I walked from door to door, I tried to understand why so much negative attention was directed towards me.

At about 7:45, I was making my way back to my house, because I had to be home by 8:00. As I walked past an alley entrance, a tall man in a black leather jacket turned, faced in my direction, and stopped. He was now only two or three steps away from me. All of a sudden, he grabbed my arm, twisted it, and pulled me into the alley.

About two garages past the alley entrance, he yelled to me, "Get up against the door, you bitch."

I immediately replied, "I'm a guy!"

He gave me a strange look and said, "Yeah, right."

He began placing his hands on my chest. While he did this, I kept insisting, "I'm a guy...I'm a guy!"

He acted as if he didn't even hear me. While he was rubbing his hands on my chest, I remember that I was not afraid of him, probably because the touch did not feel sexual or threatening to me.

I pushed him back a little and said, "I'm a guy, and I can prove it."

He stopped long enough to say, "Okay, show me."

I don't know what I was thinking about when I unbuttoned my sister's blouse, but I had to prove I was a guy.

After seeing my bare chest, he reached forward, grabbed my breasts, and said, "That's okay. I like small ones."

I yelled, "You jerk! Stop it!"

He said, "Let me see if you're a guy." Then he reached down under the short skirt and grabbed a handful of groin.

Surprised, he said, "You are a guy!"

"What do you think I've been trying to tell you?!" I yelled.

He looked both ways down the alley and said, "That's okay. We'll do it anyway."

That's the first time I can remember being afraid of him. When he next came at me, I shot the toe of my shoe forward onto his shin so hard that my foot hurt. Then I started to run as he bent over, holding his shin and swearing at me. I was only two blocks from home, and I ran as fast as I could, which was difficult since I was wearing a skirt and pumps, and carrying my precious bag of candy.

Four doors from home, I finally dared to look back. I had lost him. I stopped, caught my breath, and straightened out my clothes. My next move is something that often puzzles me now, but when you're 11 years old, and it's Halloween night, what is the most important thing? That's right—candy. I figured I only had four more chances to fill my bag.

I approached the first house. I knew the man who lived there because my brothers and sister always played near his home. When he answered the door, I said, "Trick or treat."

He said, "Uh, okay, wait a minute." When he returned, he was standing stark naked, holding a candy bar alongside his penis, saying, "Here's your trick or treat, little girl."

I yelled, "I'm a guy, you jerk!" then turned and ran home.

At home, I got undressed immediately and put on some clothes of my own.

The rest of my family was sitting around the table, talking about how much fun they had that evening. Everyone's candy was piled up while Ma and Dad picked which ones we could have and threw the others out. As everyone was happily talking and eating candy, I could only think of being trapped in the alley with that man's hands on me, and the sight of the other guy holding the candy bar by his groin.

I never told anyone. I thought I had caused these things to happen to me because I dressed like a girl. For a long time after that night, I felt as though everyone was looking at me strangely.

Whenever my friends or anyone in my family glanced at me, my response was, "What, why are you looking at me like that?"

Now I understand that none of this was my fault. If I would have known that the first guy was going to grab me...if I would have known that the other guy was going to come back to the door naked...well, *if I would have known better, I would have done better.*

Rape is sexual assault brought about by the threat or use of force. It is a crime of hatred for the control and humiliation of the victim. Rape is not committed because the rapist is sexually deprived or "horny." Rape is a crime of violence where sex is only the vehicle used to deliver the pain, control, and humiliation.

Rape is probably the most horrible crime that can happen to anyone, short of murder. Yet it is a crime in which the victim is often perceived to be the wrongdoer.

"Did you see the way she was walking?"

"Did you see how she was dressed?"

"She had on tight jeans and a low-cut sweater. She *asked* for it!"

Statements like these are commonly used when referring to a victim of rape. Why? When someone steals your car, people don't ask, "Why did the car look so nice?" When your home is burglarized, they don't say, "You shouldn't have had such a nice video recorder." When your purse is stolen, they don't say, "I bet you secretly desired someone to take your purse--you were really asking for it." So why should it be said that when a woman is raped, it is her fault?

Let's take a look at our society's attitude toward women. From an early age, young boys learn that they are supposed to be aggressive and pursue; young girls learn to be coy and passive. You can recall this television scene: several teenage girls dressed in nighties are huddled on a bed discussing "boys." The phone rings; one of the girls answers it and tells one of the others, "It's for you — it's Tommy!"

They all scream and giggle. How will she get out of this? She doesn't want to talk to him — she's too embarassed! She nervously uses the "feminine" excuse — "Tell him I'm washing my hair."

After all, she's been taught not to appear interested, even if she is. And if she isn't, she's been taught not to be rude. After years of being conditioned to behave in this manner, then a woman is raped, and people say, "Why didn't she just say no? She must have really wanted it."

Consider the advertising that tells women, "If you want love, use this product." "Get a little closer; use this deodorant." "Have shiny, bouncy, sexy hair." "Gentlemen prefer legs that are enhanced by these silky pantyhose." The female is portrayed as the seductress, the male the pursuer.

To make matters worse, rape is often the subject of "jokes."

> *"Hey, I stopped a rape from happening the other day."*
> *"Good. How'd you do it?"*
> *"I changed my mind."*
>
> *A woman runs into a police station screaming, "Grape! Grape!"*
> *A police officer sees that she has been beaten and her clothes torn off, and he says, "Ma'am, you must be mistaken, you don't mean 'grape,' you mean 'rape'."*
> *She says, "No, officer, I mean grape. You see there were a bunch of them."*

We were once in a discussion with a group of high school teachers and had been discussing child sexual assault. Everyone agreed how horrible that was, and we brought up the fact that senior citizens are raped, also. A female teacher in her mid-forties said, "Senior citizens? Boy, at that age, I'd think a woman would be lucky to get raped."

People have to understand that rape is a crime of violence, not sex. To stop rape, we must begin by stopping the rape "jokes." Rape is not a joke, and forced sex is not fun. It does not give either party sexual gratification.

To understand the impact of rape, let's examine it in the context of other crimes against the person as they are experienced by the victim. All crimes against the person can be said to be violations of the self, and, as such, they precipitate crisis reactions.

Burglary

A person usually regards his home as an extension of himself. It is, in the most primitive sense, both nest and castle. Particularly in a densely populated, highly complex environment, it is one's home that offers peace and security. Each "nest" is constructed uniquely; each is different, just as individuals are different. When that nest is befouled by a burglary, it is not so much the fact that money or possessions have been taken, but more that a part of the self has been intruded upon or violated.

Armed robbery

While in a burglary the victim is not directly involved, in armed robbery there is an encounter between the victim and the criminal. Not only is an extension of the self (property, money, etc.) taken from the victim, but he is also coercively deprived of independence and autonomy--the ability to determine one's own fate. Under the threat of violence, the victim surrenders control, and his future rests unpredictably in the hands of a "threatening other." This situation has a profound impact upon the ego of the victim.

Assault and robbery

Here is added a third affront. In addition to the loss of independence and the removal of something one sees symbolically as a part of "self," an injury is inflicted on the body, which is regarded as the envelope of the self. When the external part of the self is injured, it is painful, not only physically, but psychologically as well. The victim is left with the physical evidence to remind him that he was forced to surrender his autonomy--that he was helpless to protect or defend himself.

Forcible rape

Short of homicide, forcible rape is the ultimate violation of self. The victim is not only deprived of autonomy and control, experiencing manipulation and often injury to the envelope of the self, but there is also an intrusion of inner space, the most sacred and private repository of the self. It does not matter which bodily orifice is breached. Symbolically, they are much the same, and have, so far as the victim is concerned, the asexual significance that forceful access has been provided into the innermost source of ego.

To view rape as purely a sex crime encourages the search for possible sources of satisfaction in the experience for the victim.

Actually there is little opportunity for gratification in this context. If one focuses only on the sexual aspect, one would be tempted to believe there would be few effects of rape on women with considerable sexual experience. This is not the case. That is why promiscuous women, for whom sexual activity is frequent, will experience rape as a crisis. Even prostitutes, for whom sex is a commodity, have a need to feel a sense of control. When that sense of control is taken from any woman, her ego will suffer a profound injury. For all women, the focus is upon the intrusion and the violation of self.

Adding to the victim's distress over violation is her awareness of the moral taboos which traditionally have surrounded the sex function. Cultural myths about rape will lead her to fear how friends and relatives will react toward her, and perhaps induce guilt feelings that she surrendered to a "fate worse than death."

Chapter 2

Types of Rape

In law enforcement terms, there are two types of rape: forcible and non-forcible. Forcible rape occurs when the rapist uses physical force or a weapon to obtain his goal. Non-forcible rape occurs when the rapist uses verbal intimidation, threat, coercion, or other non-physical methods to obtain his goal.

The image that comes to mind when most people hear the word "rape" is that of a male stranger attacking a female victim. In reality, there is a large variety of situations in which rape occurs. The majority of rape victims are either related to or somehow acquainted with their attackers. Rape is not limited to a male attacker and a female victim. Anyone can rape anyone else. Let's take a look at the possibilities.

Man to man

Men rape other men for the same reasons they rape women — or power, control, domination, and humiliation. Some people refer to this male/male interaction as "homosexual rape." However, that it not necessarily an accurate term. The man that rapes another man is not always a homosexual.

The male rapist may choose a male victim because he is the only available person at the time, as, for example, in the prison environment. More often, though, a male chooses another male in an attempt to exercise the ultimate form of control over another person. In prison, the objective may be to keep the fear running high among the new inmates--to maintain the "pecking order." Outside of prison, a male might choose another male simply to serve as a target on which to assert control and inflict humiliation.

Imagine the impact on a man of being on a date and being unexpectedly jumped by two thugs who tie the girl up, beat him, force him to fellate them, rape him anally with their penises and other objects, then laugh and sneer at him--all in the presence of his girlfriend? When men hear about an incident like this one, they often say, "Well, the guy must have been some kind of wimp. A 'real' man could have defended himself." Unfair remarks such as these continue the humiliation of the victim long after the actual rape.

Woman to woman

You might wonder, how is it possible for a woman to rape a woman?

In an actual case, the victim, nineteen-year-old Sue Roberts*, left her house to purchase marijuana. On her way, she met defendant Ann Levy, whom she had known for about three years. Levy invited Roberts to accompany her to a place where some marijuana could be purchased. The building was boarded up and padlocked. After the two women smoked marijuana, Levy ordered Roberts to take off her clothes, ripping her shirt. Roberts retaliated by hitting Levy with a bottle. Levy then threatened her with a whip and ordered her to undress and scrub the floor. At that point, Joe Talbot, the co-defendant, came out of the bathroom. Levy tied Roberts' hands and feet. Both defendants undressed, and Levy ordered Sue Roberts to perform deviate sex acts on her and Talbot. Levy beat Roberts with the whip and hit her about the face with masking tape and electrical cord. Afterwards, all three fell asleep.

When they awoke the next day, Levy and Talbot again beat Roberts and then shaved her head. She was subjected to repeated beatings and forced sexual acts. Later, Levy and Talbot left, and Roberts was able to untie her bindings and flee. The physician who

---
*The names in this case have been changed.

examined Roberts in an emergency room testified at the trial that her head had been shaven; her eyes were blackened; and her body was covered with bruises, welts, and scratches.

Ann Levy didn't see Sue Roberts as a human being. She saw her as a piece of meat--something on which to vent her anger. Shaving her head and forcing her to scrub the floor were efforts to dominate the victim, in the same way that the sexual domination functioned. Ann Levy received pleasure not from the sex acts, but from inflicting mental and physical pain on the victim. Ann Levy wasn't coerced into acting this way by her male accomplice. She would have managed the situation fine by herself.

We cite this particular case not only because it demonstrates the element of control, but because it illustrates another injustice. Ann Levy was not convicted of rape because in 1984, when the incident occurred, the language of the rape law in Illinois stated that a woman could not rape another woman. Rape was defined as any penetration of the female sex organ by the male sex organ. That definition has since been reworded. Now, the sexual assault law is "gender neutral," meaning anyone, male or female, can be raped by anyone, male or female.

Woman to man

When we begin to speak about a woman raping a man, there is usually one man in the audience who responds with, "Lucky guy." He is, of course, thinking about a woman who is sexually aggressive, someone who would initiate a sexual encounter. This is not the kind of situation to which we refer at all.

Consider this scenario: A woman hitchhiker suggests to the driver that they rent a hotel room to engage in sexual activity. Once inside, she commands him to remove his clothes and lie on the bed. He's enjoying her sexual aggressiveness and does as she says. She then tells him that she would like to play a "game" and tie him up while she "gets down" on him. He thinks it's a little bit kinky, but not wanting to ruin the "mood," he agrees. After he is tied up, the woman begins to verbally abuse and humiliate him. She covers his mouth with masking tape to drown out his pleas for help. She then shoves a bottle into his anus repeatedly. He passes out from the pain. The next day, he is found dead in the hotel, having been castrated and left bleeding to death.

Does anyone still think the guy was "lucky?"

This may be an extreme example, but it shows how a woman can overpower a man by getting him to let down his defenses. In addition to seducing him into a vulnerable position, a woman could use a weapon or drugs, or she could threaten to harm a loved one.

Also included in this category are the many incidents of a grown woman sexually assaulting a young boy. Again, this violation of self is serious and traumatic, and certainly not a topic for humor or envy.

Victim to victim

In some rape cases, the attackers force the victims into sexual acts with each other. Take the case of three football players at a college in Michigan. They were invited to "party with some hot broads" by a few guys that they had seen on campus previously. Eagerly, the three athletes accepted the invitation and accompanied the other men to the "party house."

As the third football player entered the room, a guy grabbed his hair from behind, yanked his head back, and placed a large butcher knife against his throat. His cohorts then ordered the remaining two athletes to perform sexual acts on each other. This continued for some time, with all three being forced to take turns. Throughout the attack, the assailants demeaned the football players, calling them "faggots" and accusing all "jocks" of being gay. Photographs were taken and were later displayed around campus.

As it turns out, the three attackers had, at one time, been humiliated verbally in front of a group of girls by these very same football players. They had premeditated this scheme to retaliate for what had happened. The embarassment of the football players was so great that they eventually ended up leaving the university.

Man to woman

As one would expect, this type of rape is the one that happens most often. Yet there are many different situations in which it may occur. Not all rapists are strangers lurking in dark alleys. As a matter of fact, that is very seldom the case.

Acquaintance Rape occurs when a man that the woman knows or has previously met forces himself upon her sexually. He may be an angry former boyfriend, or someone the victim has no reason to fear, such as a friend of the family, a neighbor, a co-worker, the mailman, etc. In many cases, because the victim knew the person, she sidestepped her natural defenses and made herself vulnerable to the attack.

> Example: A secretary is asked by her boss to "log in some overtime" as she has many times before. Alone with her in the office, he suddenly becomes sexually suggestive and starts touching her in a "different" way. She doesn't like what is happening and becomes uncomfortable. She tries to escape the situation politely, but his suggestions become demands.

"Listen, we've worked together now for years. Don't you think it's been long enough? I know you think about me, too. Why else would you have spent all of that extra time with me?"

When she resists, he threatens her with the loss of her job. She is raped.

> Example: The trusting, unassuming suburban housewife obliges the local mailman who requests an opportunity to "come in out of the rain for a couple of minutes." Having no reason to fear or mistrust him, she offers him a cup of coffee. He comments on the house being so quiet and asks if she is home alone. Still oblivious to the danger, she replies, "As usual. Sometimes I go batty in here being by myself all day." Taking her comment as an invitation, he becomes sexually suggestive, forces her to the floor, and rapes her.

In neither of these examples did the women fight back. This lack of retaliatory response often occurs, for two reasons: the women are in shock that an acquaintance would try to rape them, and they found themselves unable to injure a person that they knew.

Date rape occurs when a boyfriend or date forces himself sexually upon his girlfriend. He may be the woman's steady boyfriend, someone she has dated previously, or someone she is dating for the first time. Physical force may or may not be used; he may rely on verbal intimidation, guilt, deception, or the use of drugs or alcohol to obtain his goal.

> Example: After two previous double-dates, Ted suggests an evening out alone with Molly, a high school classmate. She agrees, and they go to dinner and a show. After a very pleasant evening, he drives her home and walks her to the doorway. Ted asks if he may come inside for a few minutes. Molly says, "I guess so; my parents won't be home for a while yet."
>
> Molly is thinking, "Oh, a chance to be alone."
>
> Ted's unspoken reaction is, "Okay, that's the green light. A chance to get her alone."
>
> After some light necking, Ted becomes very aroused and uncontrollable, using his hands in a forceful manner. Molly's attempts to calm him down fail. He irritatingly asks, "Well, why did you invite me in here, anyway? Come on, don't tease me!" He then physically restrains her and forces her into sexual intercourse.
>
> Minutes later, Ted asks, "Did you enjoy that as much as I did?"
>
> Molly does not reply.
>
> Ted continues, "I'd better get out of here before your parents come home. What about the game Friday night? Can I see you afterwards?"
>
> Shocked by his questions and arrogant behavior, Molly can only ask herself, as many other women do in that situation, "Was I really raped?"

Since we have found that date rape occurs frequently among the high school and college students we teach, we address the ritual of dating in our seminars. We act out the "Date Scene" using the characters Tom and Mary, who could be two students anywhere.

Types of Rape

Mary has a crush on Tom, a popular guy at school. She dreams about him all the time. But it seems as if Tom doesn't know that Mary is alive. So how does Mary tell Tom that she likes him and would like to date him? Does she go up to Tom and say, "Hey, Tom, my name is Mary. I see you around school here a lot, and I'd like to go out with you Friday night. Would you care to?" And does this conversation follow?

Tom: "Mary, I think it's great that you like me, and I'm glad you asked me out."

Mary: "You don't think I'm too forward, do you?"

Tom: "Of course not. Let's be honest with each other, okay?"

Mary: "Wait a minute, Tom. I hope you don't think that I asked you out because I want to fool around. That's not what I meant. I just want to go out and have a good time, and get to know each other as friends, all right?"

Tom: "I agree. Maybe I'd want to have some type of sexual relationship in the future, but that's not what I'm interested in now. I really don't know you that well, and if we rushed into a sexual situation right away, that might ruin our friendship or just put a lot of pressure on us that we don't need now. You know, I'm really into sports and good grades, and I wouldn't want anything to put a damper on that, you know what I mean?"

Mary: "I'm glad you feel like that, Tom."

Tom: "Can I tell you something else, Mary? I feel really attracted to you, and I want to kiss you. When we go out, both of us will be worrying about when the first kiss is going to be, and we'll both be nervous. Could we kiss right now, and get it over with, so we don't have to worry about it later? Would that be all right with you?"

Mary: "That sounds like a great idea to me."

(Tom and Mary kiss briefly, and they both enjoy it.)

Tom: "That was nice, Mary. Now that we got that over with, let's decide where we want to go. Do we have to go through all of those silly games where you pretend you don't know where you want to go, and I have to be the one to..."

Mary: "Say no more, Tom. I know where I want to go. Let's go to eat at the Ninth Street Cafe. Remember, this date was my idea, so I am going to pay."

Tom: "Wow! That's really nice of you, Mary. You don't think the guys will call me a wimp or anything like that, do you?"

Mary: "Why, because I'm paying for dinner? Don't be ridiculous. And if they do say that, it's their problem, not ours. We said we're not going to play any silly games. So let's not worry about what some of your friends might say."

Tom: "Sounds great, Mary. I'll pick you up on Friday about 7:00."

Is that what happens when Mary likes Tom? OF COURSE NOT!

Mary would never approach Tom first, because then she'd be "too forward." Tom might not like that, or she might be labeled "that kind of girl." Tom would never accept Mary's invitation to pay for dinner because then he wouldn't be "cool" in front of the guys. You see, in our scenario, Tom doesn't have a chance to play his macho games and be the one to ask her and control the situation, and Mary doesn't have the chance to play all of her girlish

Types of Rape

games, namely being coy, giggly, and "hard to get." In an honest relationship like the one we described, Tom can't play "masculine," and Mary can't play "feminine."

What Mary *really* does is hang around wherever Tom goes. Tom shoots hoops at the basketball court; Mary's on the side, laughing with her friends, and going to the washroom thirteen times to comb her hair and reapply make-up.

When that method fails, Mary goes up to two of her friends and says, "You know that boy, Tom? I really like him a lot. Actually, I'm dying to go out with him. . . but don't tell anyone!"

Now Mary's friends have to go and tell Tom's friends. They won't go directly to Tom because they need an excuse to talk to Tom's friends, and this is a pretty good one. They tell Tom's friends that Mary is shy and that she likes Tom. Now it's Tom's friends' turn to deliver the message to Tom. Do you think the conversation would go like this?

Buddies: "Hey, Tom, you know that girl Mary? The one that's always watching you shoot hoops?"

Tom: "Yeah, I know her."

Buddies: "Well, we saw her nice friends today and. . ."

Tom: "Oh, those friends of hers--they're hot, aren't they?"

Buddies: "No, Tom, why would you even *think* that? They're nice girls with real nice personalities. They told us that Mary likes you and would like to date you."

Tom: "Oh, Mary's hot then. I heard Mary likes to party and really get downnnn!"

Buddies: "Come on, Tom, quit talking like a pig. Mary's just real shy. Why don't you ask her out?"

Tom: "Yeah! Should I try to get lucky, guys? I heard that she let some guys at a party take

>
> her top off, and they all felt her up. I think *I* could get something off of her, too."

Buddies: "Listen, Tom. We heard about that party. She didn't *let* them take her top off. Those guys were jerks. They did it against her will. You know it was wrong for them to do that. It wasn't her fault, and you shouldn't judge *her* by what *they* did."

Tom: "I didn't know that, guys. So you don't think I should try to score, then? How far should I go with her?"

Buddies: "Here's what you should do, Tom. If you like her, go out with her. Get to know her as a friend, respect her as a person, and then, if you want something sexual to happen, ask her. Don't ask *us* how far you should go."

Tom: "Hey, wait a minute. If I ask *her*, I ain't goin' nowhere."

Buddies: "Well, Tom, maybe that's the way it should be. After all, you don't want sex if the other person doesn't want it, do you?"

Tom: "Well, I thought that when girls said no, that they really meant yes. You mean girls don't want to be forced? They don't want to get roughed up before they have sex?"

Buddies: "Of course not, Tom. That's ridiculous. Just go out with her, and have a good time. Don't rush anything. Remember, respect her, okay?"

Tom: "All right, guys, that sounds like good advice."

Is that how Tom's buddies would talk to Tom? OF COURSE NOT!

This might be more like it.

Types of Rape 25

Buddies: "Hey, Tom! You won't believe this. Mary's hot, she's *dying* for you...she wants you bad... go get some now... go score now... don't waste any more time... GO GET HER!"

So Tom asks Mary out. She's overjoyed. Tom provides the transportation, pays for dinner, and now at the end of the evening, he drives them into the park so they can "talk."

Mary's thinking, *"Oh, I'm so lucky to be with him."*
Tom's thinking, *"I'm going to get lucky."*

Tom: "You know, Mary, I really like you a lot."

Mary: "Well, I like you, too."

Tom thinks to himself, *"That's my cue. I'm going to go for it now."* He slides his hand down between Mary's legs.

She slides his hand away gently and says, "Tom, please don't do that."

"Umm, she blocked my hand. I'd better try a different approach." Tom leans back and spreads his legs to show Mary his excitement.

"Oh my God," she thinks to herself, pretending not to notice. *"He's horny... I'd better do what my mother always says to do when a guy gets that way... I'll talk about the weather."*

Mary: "Boy, it's really HOT outside, isn't it?"

Tom: *"I knew it!! She's hot! She wants me."* Now Tom starts climbing all over her. Mary's resisting and covering up every second. Confused and irritated at her attempts to block his advances, he asks her, "What's the matter with you? I thought you liked me. You agreed to park here with me, didn't you?"

Mary: "Well, I do like you, Tom, but you're just moving too fast."

Tom decides to use a little guilt on her.

Tom: "You know, Mary, I bought you dinner, and I waited all night, and you know — everyone else is doing it. You don't want to be a little baby, do you?"

Mary: "Well, I'm not a little baby, and..."

Tom sees her weakening and decides to move on her again. He begins to kiss her forcefully. She resists, not because she doesn't want to be with him, but because he is moving at his own fast pace without even considering her feelings.

Pleading nervously, Mary says, "No, stop, Tom." (It doesn't seem to be working. Remember, he believes "no" means "yes.")

Tom becomes angry. *"I'm not going to make this a wasted evening. Who does she think she is, anyway? I thought she was hot for me. Everyone said so. Why is she playing hard-to-get? I'm going to give her what she came here for."* Tom proceeds to physically restrain Mary, remove her clothes, and rape her.

A sad part of this scenario is that Tom doesn't even believe that he raped Mary. He merely thinks that she wanted to be forced into it.

"After all, she was hot for me. I just had to give her a little push. You know, all girls like it rough."

Infamily rape or **incest** occurs when a member of the family forces himself upon another member of the family. Of course, this situation is not limited to a male-female combination, but the most frequent cases of incest that are reported involve a father or stepfather and a daughter. Many cases begin when the victim is very young and cannot yet differentiate between affection and abuse. The offender may begin with simple touching or fondling and later lead her into sexual intercourse. He may use deception ("This is how daddies show they love their daughters") or intimidation ("If you tell anyone about this, Mommy will think you're bad") to force compliance. Finally, the child may gather the courage to tell her mother or another person only to find that no action will be taken. Many times the wife of the abuser is dominated or abused herself, and she fears the repercussions of upsetting him. If the authorities are notified, the entire family structure will be shattered, with the child possibly ending up in a foster home with strangers--a frightening thought to any child and mother.

For these reasons, infamily rape is perhaps the most emotionally traumatizing type of rape. There is no easy way out. The victim is constantly exposed to the abusive environment. She grows up confused about her own sexuality and unable to handle relationships with others. Many victims are driven to drastic measures to escape--alcohol, drugs, or even suicide.

Marital rape occurs when a husband rapes his wife. There are no national figures available on marital rape because in many states it is not against the law for a husband to rape his wife. As a matter of fact, "marital rape" is a contradiction in terms to many people--including a priest at a Catholic high school in Indiana where we delivered our workshop. These people have the notion that when a woman marries a man, she becomes his property. Of course, we strongly disagree. Marital rape most often occurs in a battered wife syndrome. In that type of marriage, the woman is dominated in every facet of her life by the man. She usually has very low self-esteem, and he reinforces that notion. The husband will beat her, then force her to succumb to his wishes for sex. This situation is not limited to low-income homes or poorly educated families. The problem exists in many financially stable, well-educated, professional families. However, these women are not as apt to report it.

Gang rape occurs when two or more men rape a woman. They may be strangers to the woman or someone with whom she is acquainted. Quite possibly this is the most brutal type of attack because all of the participants take turns on the victim. Think about how competitive some men are when they get together. In a gang rape situation, they often try to outdo each other.

"I did it to her this way."
"I made her do it like this."
"I kicked her when I was done."
"Well, I shoved this bottle into her."
"I poured a beer on her afterwards."

The following incident happened to a girl (we'll call Janet) when she was seventeen. Janet's parents were very strict with her, never allowing her to date. She had a difficult time getting her parents to trust her. Since she couldn't go out with boys, Janet devised a plan to spend time with a boy named Joe that she liked. She'd have a party at her house. *"All I have to do is convince my parents that it will be okay. I'll be reasonable. It won't be like I'm going out. I'll have the party down in the basement, and I could invite Joe and his friends and all of my friends."*

Janet proposes the idea to her parents, finally getting them to agree. Janet's friends are shocked. "Wow, Janet! How did you swing that with your parents? You'd better make sure nothing goes wrong, or they'll never let you have a party again!"

Janet agrees, "Yeah, they'd probably never even let me out again!" The big night arrives. Everything is going well for Janet, except that Joe doesn't seem to pay much attention to her. He stays with his friends who seem to be huddled together, as if they were in on some deep, dark secret. Whenever Joe looks over at Janet, she smiles and melts.

Towards the end of the evening, Joe compliments Janet on the great party and tells her that he and his friends have to be leaving.

"I really wish you could stay longer, Joe. If your friends have to go, maybe you could stay."

Joe turns to his buddies in the corner and winks at them. They all start to laugh. "What's so funny?" Janet asks. Joe shrugs it off. "Oh, nothin'. They're a little weird tonight. Maybe it was too much to drink. They get a little wild. Well, I'll be seeing you, Janet."

"Okay, Joe. I'll see you around school. Bye."

After the party breaks up, Janet begins to clean the basement so her parents won't see all the beer cans lying around. She keeps thinking about how this successful party will convince her parents that she is really responsible. They might even let her have another party, or better yet--begin dating boys.

Janet has only one regret--that things might have gone a little better with Joe. She'd hardly gotten a chance to talk to him. She begins to daydream and fantasize. She thinks of Joe ringing the doorbell, saying he forgot something and then admitting that he really came to see her...that he couldn't stand being away from her.

Just then, the doorbell rings. Janet pulls the curtain to the side. It's Joe!

Janet opens the door. "What happened?"

"Well, Janet, since I got a ride with the guys, I had to leave with them. But I really wanted to spend more time with you, so I convinced them to bring me back."

"Are they here?" Janet questions.

"Yeah, they're in the car. But it's really cold outside. If I come in, could they come, too? They could watch TV in the next room while we talk."

"I guess it's all right. But only if they're real quiet; I don't want my parents to know I'm down here alone with four guys."

"Thanks, Janet, you're cool. I'll tell them to come in."

Janet and Joe are sitting on the couch close together, talking, giggling, and enjoying each other's company. They start to kiss. Joe's buddies walk into the room and ask if they can sit down on the couch for a while. Without waiting for Janet's reply, they plop down next to her and Joe. Joe becomes silent as if he knows something is about to happen. Janet looks quizzically at Joe, but he says nothing.

"Hey, Joe, you're busy in here making out, and we're sitting all lonely in the other room. Got any company for us, Janet?"

Janet feels uncomfortable and starts to get up. One of Joe's buddies yanks her down by the arm and starts kissing her! Joe does nothing to stop him. The other two boys begin to feel her breasts and kiss her all over.

"Joe, what's going on?" Janet cries. Joe sits quietly.

"Hey, Joe, what's the matter?" asks one of the guys. "Come on, get in on some of this. You said you wanted to do it. You chickening out now?"

Joe pauses, thinking about what the guys will say if he doesn't go along. He makes a feeble attempt to stop them when he sees that Janet is terrified and struggling.

"What's the matter, Joe? You ain't ever been screwed before? Come on, we got a *party broad!*"

Joe's buddy goes over to the telephone and rips out the cord. He returns, and they proceed to bind Janet with it. They allow Joe to be first to rape her because she was his "catch." Joe forces his penis into her and rapes her. The others follow, adding their own sexual acts, orally and anally penetrating her. They all pour beer on her when they are done and then untie her. They leave Janet in a heap on the floor.

Janet never screams for help, even though her parents are right upstairs. She thinks that if they come down and see what is happening that they will never let her out again, that she will be grounded for life... that they will blame her... that they will press charges, and everyone will know what happened to her... that Joe will get in trouble. *She's still thinking about Joe's feelings.*

One week passes, and it's Friday again. Janet has received several phone calls, but no one is on the other end of the line. She wishes she could avoid answering, but her parents are out, and if they call, they would expect her to be home.

About 9:00 p.m., the doorbell rings. Janets opens the door to find Joe's three buddies, one of them carrying a small duffel bag. She is shocked. "What are you doing here?"

"We brought our own telephone wire this time. We thought you'd like to party again. Joe didn't want to come, but we thought we'd come anyway. We know your parents aren't home. We've been calling all night to see. Did you know it was us?"

Janet slams the door and runs upstairs.

Stranger rape occurs when the attacker is unknown to the woman. The stranger rapist chooses his victim by her accessibility, availability, and vulnerability. The attacker may stalk his victim by following her or marking her daily routine. This is not the most common type of rape, but it's the most believable. It reinforces the myths many people have about rapists. Stranger rape is frequently portrayed on television and in the movies. It receives wide newspaper coverage, whereas other, more common types of rape do not. Imagine a headline that reads, "Woman Raped by her Date." Women feel safer believing that only strangers commit rape because they think they can avoid the situation. *"That would never happen to me; I never go out at night alone."* It also helps them to justify someone else's rape. *"She asked for it by leaving her car doors unlocked."* Most women prefer to believe that they could never be attacked by someone they know.

Chapter 3

Who Rapes...And Why

Most rapes are performed by a male upon a female. Although we have acknowledged that rape can occur in a variety of male-female configurations, we will be focusing here on the most common situation of a man raping a woman.

Men who rape are not outwardly noticeable by any special characteristics. When we are asked to describe the typical rapist, we reply: It could be a male of any size, shape, age, race, or class. He can strike any time or anywhere. He has no preference when picking his victim. His physical appearance cannot be classified. He could quite possibly be that "nice boy next door."

Our research indicates that the rapist has often been the victim of child abuse. He may have experienced early childhood sexual relations with an older woman. He may have been emotionally, physically, and/or sexually dominated by a female, most likely his mother or female guardian. He was probably left confused and angered. Some rapists have deep-rooted fears of being homosexual.

In their book *The Rapist File*, Sussman and Bordwell found that most rapists were the sons of mothers who showed them little or no love. They were constantly frustrated in attempts to please their mothers and receive their approval. They often saw their fathers dominated by these women.

One man said his father worked ten hours a day and then came home to do the dishes, vacuum the floor, and clean the house. There was never a hot meal waiting for him. In the rapist's words, "Mom sat on her butt all day."

Another rapist had lived in a household of women. He was the only son and had two sisters. The girls got all the attention, and he was always considered the "black sheep" of the family. They verbally abused him and dominated him, yet expected him to perform all the physical tasks for the household. He felt as though he had been "used."

Men like these view rape as the ultimate form of retaliation — a chance to finally obtain power and control.

We have found that there are three broad categories into which most rapists fall.

The power rapist

The *power rapist* is sometimes referred to as the *sexually inadequate rapist*. This person needs reassurance of his manhood; he tries to prove to himself that he is a man by taking control of a woman. The power rapist:

a. fears homosexuality

b. works hard at arousing victim; wants her to enjoy the sexual act

c. directs victim's activity to create his fantasy

d. may be impotent; requires assistance of victim to maintain an erection

e. needs verbal encouragement; tells victim what to say

f. verbalizes; engages in extensive conversation

g. asks personal questions in an effort to create intimacy

h. exhibits a pathetic need for affection — occasionally victim responds sympathetically to his needs

i. may be well-educated, white-collar, in family crisis

j. has guilt feelings and sorrow, needs to confess, easy to apprehend

The power rapist will not often use physical brutality, but he will physically restrain the victim or verbally intimidate her. This type of rapist doesn't want to believe that he is committing rape. That is why he'll try to make the victim enjoy the sexual act. He believes that if she seems to receive sexual pleasure, that it really won't be rape. The power rapist thinks that "real" rapists are sick, perverted men waiting for helpless victims in a dark alley. He believes he would never fall into that category, because he is just an "average" guy.

The anger rapist

The *anger rapist* is sometimes referred to as the *assaultive rapist*. If any man would fit the popular connotation of a rapist, this one probably would. He often acts after a drinking bout or in a drug-induced state. The anger rapist blames his frustrations and hard times on all women. Whenever he encounters misfortune, he seeks to vent his anger on a woman. The anger rapist:

a. approaches the victim by striking her or physically restraining her
b. tears at her clothing and grabs her private parts
c. uses vile and abusive language
d. is socially isolated; lives in a world of sexual fantasy in which he controls and dominates women
e. may have a previous record including instances of drinking and committing acts of assault
f. has a low frustration tolerance; anything the victim says or does angers him and makes him violent
g. acts in a manner to shock the victim
h. strikes sporadically and frequently

The sadistic rapist

The *sadistic rapist* enjoys inflicting mental and physical pain on the victim. His crimes are usually well publicized because they involve bizarre and deviate sexual acts, often resulting in murder or mutilation. The sadistic rapist:

a. intimidates and totally dominates the victim
b. ties and binds the victim to cause torturing and suffering
c. demands degrading sexual acts, such as anal and oral penetration; often uses an object to rape victim
d. acts out hostilities
e. is bright and elusive; may be successful in life, financially stable
f. has a superior attitude
g. frequently kidnaps victim
h. may dismember and mutilate victim after sex act
i. often murders victim

In a case that received wide media attention, Larry Singleton was found guilty of raping Maria, a 15-year-old girl, and then hacking off both of her arms with an axe. Thinking she was dead, he left her in a ditch. The girl managed to walk and crawl to get help. Larry Singleton was found guilty of four charges: forcible rape, kidnapping, attempted murder, and mayhem (mutilation).

Looking closely at the three types of rapists, one can see that they are all driven by a need to dominate, not by a need to release sexual tension. The rapist does not go looking for a woman because he has a desire to have sex. The sex act is simply the means by which he controls his victim.

Chapter 4

Order in Which a Rape Occurs

There are four stages in which most rapes occur. Some of these stages may pass unnoticed by the victim. Many rapes could be prevented if more women understood how a rape happens and were able to identify a situation as a potential rape before it got to the final stage.

1. The visual attack

A *visual attack* occurs when the woman is being watched or stared at in a suggestive or demeaning manner. It is a glance that lingers way past the norm. Many women describe it by saying, "He was undressing me with his eyes," or "It felt as if he were looking right through me."

The visual attack is usually intended to embarass the woman. Instead of feeling complimented, she feels degraded. It may also make her feel frightened. In some cases, the woman seems to be unaware of the visual attack, or she may appear to disregard or overlook it.

2. The verbal attack

A *verbal attack* is a suggestive or demeaning comment which follows the visual attack. This comment may be outwardly vile or abusive (in which case it can be very frightening), or it may be subtly coy in the form of a *double entendre* — a "cute" remark that you can take two ways. ("Oooh, you're really hot, aren't you, babe? I mean, it's really warm in here, isn't it?") The verbal attack is never mistaken for a compliment. It does not leave the woman feeling flattered, but rather disgusted.

3. The physical attack

The *physical attack* is defined as "any forward movement towards you from one-step-away or less." It may be a simple touch or "accidental" bump against the woman. It may be more obvious, in the form of a grab, push, shove, or punch. Let's examine the legal terms that are used to describe a physical attack.

A person commits a *battery* if he intentionally or knowingly, without legal justification, makes physical contact of an insulting or provoking nature with an individual.

A person commits an *assault* when, without lawful authority, he engages in conduct which places another person in reasonable apprehension of receiving a *battery*.

> Example: Jim gets into an argument with Ron and takes a punch at him, but misses. Jim's buddies restrain him from any further action. He is guilty of assault. Had he connected, it would have been a battery.

> Example: Joe, enraged at Bill, backs him against a wall (without touching him) and fires a loaded pistol at him. The pistol jams and does not fire. Joe is guilty of attempted murder. He is also guilty of assault, in that he has put Bill in reasonable apprehension of receiving a battery.

Let's review: the *intent* to use force for the injury of another person is *assault*; the actual use of force is *battery*. Battery includes assault; hence the two terms are commonly combined in the term *assault and battery*. When the threat or use of a weapon is involved, it is called *aggravated assault and battery*.

In the crime of rape, the physical attack, like the verbal attack, may be blunt and obvious, or subtle and suggestive. It's easy to realize what's going on when the attacker grabs a woman by the breasts, slaps her face, and begins pressing himself against her. On the other hand, the attack may be more difficult to assess. Sometimes, subtle physical attacks may occur over a period of time before the actual sexual assault is made. A friend's father may brush his hand against a girl every time he helps her on with her coat. A woman may notice that lately her boss continues to hover over her desk, at first touching her shoulder, then progressing to other areas of her body. Any time a man invades a woman's "space," or a radius of two to three feet, making her feel threatened or violated, she should recognize the situation as a potential physical attack.

4. The sexual assault

The *sexual assault* will immediately follow the physical attack. If the victim is being badly beaten, the sexual asault will usually bring an end to the beating. The sexual assault can vary from sexual intercourse, to anal intercourse, to oral copulation, to deviate sexual acts. The sexual act may be traumatic for the victim, but it is often the least important part of the rape for the rapist. In some cases, the rapist will not maintain an erection, or will not ejaculate. He does not receive his pleasure from the sexual act *per se*, but rather from the humiliation that it causes the victim.

5. Physical or verbal intimidation

After the sexual assault takes place, the rapist will again use *physical or verbal intimidation* to further dominate the victim. Not content with merely forcing the victim to perform sexual acts, the rapist often resumes beating the victim, or he makes her perform other demeaning tasks, such as grovel and beg for more sex, bathe him, scrub the floor, or cook some food.

In a rape that happened in Chicago, the victim was verbally threatened into submission. After the sexual assault, she was allowed to get dressed and was directed to sit in a chair which the rapist provided for her directly across from him.

She was told, "Stare at this face. Remember it. You won't tell anyone now, will you?" The moment she pulled her eyes away, he violently punched her in the face. After picking her up from the floor and returning her to the sitting position, he again demanded that she keep her eyes on his face.

As soon as her eyes would drift away, he would beat her. The violent scene continued relentlessly until the next thing she saw was a nurse in a hospital emergency room.

As in this case, the physical or verbal intimidation that occurs after the sexual attack often has the objective of ensuring that the victim will dare not testify against the rapist. At other times, it seems to function as a continuation of the pleasure that the attacker receives from total domination, and it may not end until the victim is dead or unconscious.

Chapter 5

A Woman's Options

Now that we have discussed what rape is, who the rapist might be, and how a rape happens, the next logical question would be, "What should a woman do if she is attacked?" There really is no one answer to that question. What may work in one situation may not work in another. A technique that is effective on a power rapist may be totally ineffective on an anger rapist. We believe in being prepared to use several options.

Submission

One choice is to *submit* — give in to the attack and do what the rapist wants. This is not an attractive option, but if your life is in danger, and submitting seems to be the only way to stop the physical attack, it is an honorable and reasonable choice. Each year, hundreds of thousands of forcible rape victims felt they had no other recourse but to submit. We cannot tell them that they did the wrong thing. If they are alive to talk about the experience, then they made the right decision. They were not murder victims; they are *survivors*.

A woman who submits should not feel guilty for having *consented*. Let's differentiate here between submitting and consenting. Consenting to sex means that the woman wants to participate. Submitting means that she felt there was nothing else to do because she feared for her life or was in some other way intimidated.

Passive resistance

Another choice is *passive resistance* — trying to outsmart the rapist until you have discouraged him, escaped, or given yourself time to consider other options. Passive resistance may be effective in a non-violent situation, possibly one in which the attacker is known to you. It would be less effective against a stranger or a violent rapist. There are several ways passive resistance can be attempted.

Many women respond to an attack by *crying, begging,* or *pleading* with the attacker. Although often this is precisely the reaction the rapist most enjoys, and at other times, it may enrage the attacker, it can be used successfully in some cases. It is not an option which we highly recommend because of its low effectiveness rate, but, as always, it is up to you to decide what will work in your situation.

Sometimes you may attempt to *deceive* the attacker. You may give excuses as to why he should not rape you. "I'm diseased." "I'm pregnant." "I'm menstruating." "My boyfriend's waiting in that car over there." Chances are that the rapist will recognize such simplistic statements as ploys. Deception can be an effective tool to use while you bide time for an escape.

> Example: During a house party, a woman goes upstairs to use the bathroom. A man who's been staring at her all evening, visually attacking her, slips in behind her and locks the door. He has a strange look on his face, smiles coyly, and says, "Hey, baby, we've finally got a chance to be alone. I've seen the way you've been looking at me all night. Let's get it on." Without hesitation, he begins to paw her and kiss her forcefully. He's a large man, and she doesn't think she can successfully defend herself against him. Taking into consideration his confident attitude about his sexual prowess, she says, "You know--you're right. I do want you. But let's not do it here--there's no place to get comfortable. Let's go to one of the bedrooms." His ego boosted, he replies, "All right, baby, let's go." As

soon as he opens the door, she bolts out of the room and screams as loudly as possible.

This plan could have backfired. The attacker might not have agreed to move to the bedroom, and then the woman would have given him the "green light" to proceed. Changing strategy and telling him no would be difficult after just saying yes.

Another form of passive resistance is the use of *vulgar* or *"unfeminine" behavior*. It has been suggested by some rape prevention advocates that the woman pick her nose, vomit, urinate, or even pass wind in an attempt to "gross out" and discourage the attacker. We have even heard women told to drop down on all fours, start barking like a dog, foam at the mouth, and spit at the attacker. We do not recommend these techniques at all. The theory behind their use is that if you can disgust the rapist, then he won't want to have sex with you. We believe that the rapist doesn't primarily want to have sex with you; the rapist wants to control you and force you to do something against your will. In contrast, if a woman is about to engage in sexual relations with her loving partner, and she suddenly starts burping, throwing up, urinating, and passing wind, it might surely turn her lover off. But we're not talking about a beautiful relationship between consenting adults. We're talking about forced sexual acts where one partner is unwilling. Seeing his victim urinate would most likely be an added bonus to a rapist: "I got her so scared she wet her pants!" There are more effective resistance techniques to use.

The most popular and effective form of passive resistance is what we call the *strong definite "no"* or *assertiveness*. In as loud and forceful a voice as possible, tell the attacker in no uncertain terms that you do not want the attack to happen. Shout "NO!" "STOP!" "HANDS OFF!" Assertiveness works only if you apply it with confidence and you are not afraid of embarassing the person. In some cases, it won't matter how assertive you are; the attacker simply won't be affected by your verbal counter-attack.

Fighting back

The third option in the event of an attack is to *fight back*. Using self-defense techniques, strike or kick the attacker's vital

Fighting back

The third option in the event of an attack is to *fight back*. Using self-defense techniques, strike or kick the attacker's vital areas. Self-defense does not mean struggling. Struggling is ineffective physical resistance, and may only serve to anger the rapist or entice him. Fighting back means to do whatever it takes to stop the attacker--scratch at his face, gouge at his eyes, kick his groin, stomp on his foot, kick his shin, grab his testicles, pull his hair, bite at whatever comes near your mouth, or shove both of your hands into his face. Running away is a form of fighting back, too. Yelling to turn your fear into anger is fighting back. Fighting back includes all counter-attacking measures.

Let's examine the three options as they apply to an incident that happened to a student of ours in a Chicago suburb.

While on her way home from work, the high school girl was forced in between two houses on the street where she lived. A masked assailant pushed her violently against the building. He became brutal very quickly.

She recounts, "I didn't know what to think or do. He slapped me across the face so hard I was in a state of shock. He told me to take off my coat, and I did. He slapped me again and told me to take off my 'cute little top' because he wanted to see my breasts. He was talking filthy to me.

"He said, 'Let me see those babies, you little bitch.' I took off my top. He told me to put my hands on top of my head and leave them there. If I moved them, he would hit me again. He started to feel me up, and as he was doing this, I was trying to think of what to do. It seemed like it was an eternity before he showed me the gun he had in his coat pocket. I saw it. It was a real gun, a pistol. I knew that, because my father has lots of guns.

"After showing me the gun, he laid it against my shoulder, neck, and cheek. I knew I had only a few choices. I thought that if I did what he wanted, maybe, just maybe, he wouldn't shoot me, and it would be over. I tried talking to him. I told him, 'Please don't do this.' I begged him, but the more I did this, the more he rubbed my crotch and chest.

"Then he said, 'Now, it's your turn, bitch,' and told me to take

"Why did you strike him? You were giving in. You tried to talk your way out, but all of a sudden, you decided to strike?" "Yes, I decided to fight. The last thing I heard was the gun click, but it didn't fire. He was screaming and yelling. I ran back to work two blocks away. I didn't even know if he was following me. I didn't want to run home, because my Mom was alone, and I was afraid for her.

"People at work were shocked when I ran in with no clothes on the top of my body. Someone gave me a coat; someone else called the police. But the guy was gone—no clues except the shaving of skin the hospital took from underneath my fingernails and the description I had given to the police. When I was in the emergency room, they bandaged my eye, and I went home.

"Three weeks later, the local police called and asked me to come to the station for a line-up. When I entered the dark room, there he was with a patch over his left eye. I guess he had just attacked and raped another girl not far from my home the same way he had done to me. The girl, the victim, said he pulled the trigger on the gun five or six times and laughed when no bullets came out. He had sexually assaulted her, and then he intimidated her. He told her she did it just for nothing; there were no bullets." The girl telling this story was able to use all three of her choices. At first, she planned to submit. Secondly, she tried to talk her way out. Finally, she got so angry and in her words "grossed out" that she decided to fight back. She was able to adopt a strategy which allowed her to prevent completion of the sexual assault.

As black belts and masters of karate and self-defense, we find ourselves open to the same options as anyone else. We want to relate to you an incident that happened to us several years ago.

We have two children (Dan's natural children, Marie's stepchildren)--a girl named Brandi who was six years old at the time, and a boy, Daniel Joseph (D.J.), who was four years old at the time. As soon as the kids could walk, we trained them in karate and self-defense. D.J. is the kind of karate student who enjoys throwing the striking or punching techniques. Our daughter Brandi is the opposite--she loves to do any and all kicking techniques.

At this time in their lives, the kids, especially D.J., had a difficult time separating fantasy from reality. He thought that cars could jump over each other and "crash in" and that no one would be hurt. He thought the superheroes were real, and so on. Everything that D.J. said or did had to do with the fictional cartoon character, HE-MAN, from the Masters of the Universe comic and cartoon series. When HE-MAN was needed to stop crime with his powers, he would simply lift his mighty sword to the heavens, and in a powerful voice, would say, "I HAVE THE POWER." Within seconds, he would transform into a superhuman being with muscles bulging out of every part of his body. He would then save the world.

Now, when we say everything with D.J.'s life was HE-MAN, we mean *everything* was HE-MAN. He would cajole us into playing HE-MAN constantly. Marie would be Teela, the Warrior Princess; Dan would be karate Skeletor, the evil Destructor; Brandi would be another evil force; and D.J., would, of course, be the one to raise his plastic sword up to the heavens and receive the power so he could destroy us all.

During one weekend that the kids were spending with us, we purchased a new (to us) Lincoln Continental. We washed and waxed the car in preparation for a visit to Nana (Grandma) Mary's house to pick her up so she could accompany us to the zoo. We strapped the kids into the car with the seat belts. Brandi had her Cabbage Patch doll, and D.J. had his Masters of the Universe action figures and, of course, his plastic sword.

Nana Mary lives in a beautiful "re-habbed" home in a not-so-nice neighborhood fifteen minutes from the Chicago Loop. It's a crowded area with the usual riffraff making its share of trouble. As our shiny white Lincoln pulled into the only parking space within 100 feet of her house, we heard a deep rumbling sound coming from the other end of the street. Then it appeared: *The Car.* It looked like the remnants of a '63 Chevy four-door--blue, except for one of the doors, which was red. *The Car* had no windshield, the back window was shattered, there was no muffler, and the springs and shocks must have been broken because the car was tilting. On one side, in fluorescent paint, was written "MAD MAX."

At once, *The Car* came directly towards the front end of our car and just missed hitting us, turning away at the last minute. Before we could even react, it spun around in the middle of the street and headed towards the rear end of our car, again just missing us. It screeched around another time and was then facing us.

Inside were three young Hispanic *gentlemen* obviously amused with the fact that they had just terrorized us. They were screaming something in Spanish, and although we had no idea what they were saying, we knew it wasn't pleasant. Their hand signals were clear enough to interpret, however.

D.J., confident in the back seat, said, "Don't worry, Dad. Next time they come, just hit the turbo power and jump over them like 'Kit' on 'Knight Rider'." He began to signal for Kit, the talking car, by speaking into his imaginary wrist radio.

The Car was just sitting there, rumbling, while the men inside stopped to drink a bottle of whiskey. Suddenly, one of them yelled out, "Hey, we want the little broad in the back!" They were talking about our daughter Brandi!

They screeched the tires, and smoke rose from the street. As they pulled away, they threw the whiskey bottle at our car, splattering it on the hood. *The Car* was moving in a direct line towards our front fender. They smashed into us with a tremendous impact. For a second, we were silent. Before we could take another breath, D.J. unbuckled his seat belt, raised his plastic sword above his head, and hollered, "I HAVE THE POWER!" He began to swing his sword threateningly towards *The Car*.

With that, Brandi pushed him down, and leaning on the back of our seats, started throwing karate kicks into the air. "Do this one, Daddy!" she shouted, as she demonstrated a front kick.

Then she added, "Wait, I've got a better idea. . . send Marie!" D.J. agreed. "Yeah. Search and destroy, Marie!" Again, before Dan or I could react, the three thugs fled the scene.

Let's assess the situation. In our car, we had Dan, a 4th degree black belt, police training instructor, 1978 American Karate

Association Kickboxing Champion, and "Skeletor." Also in the car was Marie, a self-defense expert, karate black belt, and "Teela Warrior Princess." In the back seat, we had Brandi, who thought she was Kung-Fu-Mama, and D.J. who honestly believed he was HE-MAN, Master of the Universe.

We could have pursued any of the three options we discussed earlier in this chapter. We could have fought back. It would have been a pleasure to have jumped out of our car and beaten those three hoodlums to a pulp. But fighting back seemed inappropriate at the time. We were sure the thugs had no regard for property, nor probably for human life. And we had the children to think about. We had no idea what those men were capable of doing.

We also could have gotten out of the car and tried passive resistance, politely asking them to show us an insurance card. Or we could have calmly explained to them that we were trained self-defense experts, and that we could hurt them if they didn't stop.

We chose to submit. We sat in the car, got a description of the vehicle, and took down the license plate number.

When we related this story at a college, a student said to Dan, "You fag! You mean, you're a black belt, and you let them do that to you in front of your wife and kids?" He asserted that Dan should have defended everyone's "honor." Upon hearing the aftermath of the incident, however, he understood the appropriateness of Dan's restraint.

We drove to the nearest police station and reported the incident. As it turned out, The Car was a stolen vehicle. The day before, these men had robbed a liquor store and shot and killed the clerk. If we had confronted the men, we quite possibly could have been shot. That wouldn't have defended anyone's honor!

As we look back on that incident, we know we made the right decision. Because the men hadn't harmed us personally--only our property--we chose to submit to the attack. If they had attacked our bodies, our response would have been different. Actually, being skilled in self-defense had no bearing on the choice we made at the time. We came out of the situation alive and unhurt, and that is what matters.

Chapter 6

Self-Defense Techniques

We define self-defense as "the ability to physically defend oneself against danger, attack, or personal injury by using your body as a weapon." Self-defense includes learning physical maneuvers, but it also involves an attitude. It relies 10% on technique and 90% on *intestinal fortitude.* You have to have determination – the will to protect yourself.

Put aside all of your negative "what if?" questions and "I can't" assertions. We will not focus on what you can't do, but rather on what you can do. Do not dismiss self-defense, saying "I'm not big enough," or "I'm not strong enough." Say to yourself, "I'm going to use every ounce of my body weight and strength in my counter-attack, because only *I* can save *me.*"

You must use self-defense with the idea in your mind that IT WILL WORK. If you think it won't, then it probably won't. If you're afraid to hurt the person, then attempting self-defense will only prove dangerous to you. So, right now, let's separate the passive, submissive female from the assertive, strong-willed woman who knows she is special and is ready to fight to defend herself.

No one else can prepare you to use self-defense. No one else is going to be able to practice self-defense for you. It's just like getting in shape. Nobody can lose the weight for you. Nobody can do the exercises for you. You have to be the one to do the work to achieve this goal. It's not easy to lose weight, just like it isn't easy to become adept at self-defense. But it can be done!

When discussing self-defense, some people say "anything goes." That's true to an extent--you should do anything you can that will work--but there are some techniques that simply are not effective. There is no sense in wasting your energy performing them. Beating on the attacker's chest or slapping into his body will simply tire you out and anger him. We will explain and show you photographs of some much more effective techniques.

Most of the self-defense methods we advocate will include open-hand strikes or kicks directly into the attacker's vital areas. These are the areas concentrated along the center of the body: face or mask area, solar plexus (the pit of the stomach), and groin.

You are never really going to be "ready" for someone to attack you. It will almost always come as a surprise. However, if you are prepared enough to have considered your options ahead of time, you can successfully defend yourself. Every situation is different, but determination of the timing and the amount of force you use should center around one question, "Will I be able to escape?" In other words, "Will this strike or kick stop the attack long enough so I can escape?" Your objective is not to beat the attacker or kill him. You only want to get away.

The eyes are the most vulnerable and vital area to strike in an opponent of any size or strength. Direct contact with your fingers into the eyes will cause the most possible damage with the least amount of force. It does not require brute strength to harm the eyes. You know how much pain you experience when a mere speck of dust or an eyelash flies into your eye. You simply have to stop whatever you are doing to remove the foreign object.

We are often asked about the effectiveness of delivering a palm hand strike into the person's nose. "Is it true that if you hit with the heel of your palm directly into the person's nose that you could break his nose, shove the cartilage into his head, and kill him instantly?" The answer to the question is: Yes, you could break his nose, but no, he won't die instantly. People do not die *instantly* unless you shoot them with a cannon or similar weapon. This strike could break the assailant's nose, but that might not necessarily stop him. Some men can take a punch in the nose quite well. Rather than just concentrating on the small area of the nose, it is much better to aim for the eyes. Even if you don't hit with all of your fingers, it takes just *one* finger into someone's eyes to cause damage.

Hitting into the face or eyes will cause the attacker's body to move backwards, away from you. Another benefit of this technique is that receiving a blow to the eyes will force the attacker's hands to his face. You will accomplish two things: getting his hands off of you, and forcing his body backwards, thereby putting distance between the two of you.

Even a tiny baby knows to strike for the eyes when he feels threatened. Have you ever held someone else's baby, rocking him back and forth gently, and then put your face too close to his? That baby stuck out his petite little fingers and shoved them directly into your face or eyes. He didn't fool around with useless techniques. He did what his natural instincts told him to do. And it worked, didn't it?

Some women say they can't imagine ramming their fingers into someone's eyes. It sounds too painful and violent. We can learn a lesson from that baby. He didn't know *he wasn't supposed to be violent*. He didn't believe he was *too small to fight back*. He didn't care that *you might get angry* if he defended himself. He didn't use any of those excuses. The attacker does not care about you. Why should you care about him? When someone wants to harm you, you'd better be sure that you're going to do whatever it takes to stop him. Hands Off: I'm Special!

When we discuss self-defense techniques, we will concentrate on three basic distances between you and the attacker: one-step-away, half-a-step-away, and in-close. Most people will maintain a distance of at least one step away from another person. This territory, which we refer to as your personal "space," is off-limits to others. If someone invades that "space" against your will, you have the right to defend yourself. If you are able to tell that someone is about to invade your space, be prepared to fight.

How might someone get a half-a-step-away from you if you always keep that one-step-away distance? It could happen if the

Figure 1

person surprised you, came running at you, backed you against a wall, grabbed you from behind and spun you around, or if you knew the person and let him into your space.

The strike from one-step-away is called a *thrust into the eyes*. You must open your hand and contract the muscles, starting at the fingertips, through the hand, down past the wrist, through the entire forearm and elbow, into the bicep, and connecting into the shoulder. The thrust gains its power from stepping into it and thrusting all of your weight forward. You step forward with the same leg, same hand (in order to gain distance), and throw your body weight over the front leg. (see Figure 1) The total contraction of your body, combined with your weight moving forward, will form a devastating weapon at your disposal. After your fingers hit the eyes, penetrate past the surface area until the attacker's head pushes backward. Yell, "NO!" loudly, as you perform the technique.

A second hand strike is called a *snap into the eyes*. This strike is performed from a distance of a half-a-step-away. Because the attacker is so close, you won't be able to gain much power. You don't have the room to step in and gain momentum like you do for the thrust. So the snap strike will have to gain its power from the speed of its delivery and the ability to recoil the hand upon the point of impact.

The hand and fingers must be positioned in an open and tense fashion just as in the thrust strike. However, you only take a short step, snap your hand out into his eyes, and bring your hand back (the recoil), while yelling, "NO!" as loudly as you can. (see Figure 2) You must recoil your hand so the person won't grab it.

Remember, this strike doesn't have the power of the thrust. On the thrusting technique, even if the person did grab your hand, the force of your body weight coming at him would be sufficient to complete the strike. But the snap doesn't have that power; you need speed to work to your advantage.

Figure 2

If the assailant grabs one of your arms and pulls you towards him, your natural reaction would be to immediately pull your arm away from him. (see Figure 3) This may work. However, if he has a strong hold on your arm, you will only be playing tug-of-war, with your arm as the rope. The best way to defend against this attack is to let him pull you towards him. Use his weight to your advantage. Let him pull you, but simultaneously, step in and snap your hand out into his eyes. If the attacker pulls you down as he falls, get up and run!

The next strike is called a *scratch across face and eyes* and is executed from a distance of in-close. If the assailant grabs you in close and pulls you toward him, lift your elbows and tuck them in. If you don't, your arms will be outstretched and your hands unable to hit his face. Open up your hands, tighten your palm, slap as hard as you can to the attacker's eardrum, then rip your fingers across his temple, eyes, and nose while yelling "NO!" Scratch across the face with alternating hands--right, left, right. (see Figures 4 and 5) You do not need long nails, as you are not scratching like you would scratch an itch. You are still trying to get your

SEXUAL ASSAULT

Figure 3

fingers into the eyes--using the pads of your fingers, not your nails. If you have long nails, that's fine, but if your nails are extremely long, they could possibly hinder you by bending back and causing you pain. But, think about it--if you hit the person so hard in the face and eyes that your fingernails bent back, that would mean that you must have done some damage to his eyes!

The scratch is the most effective and most often used technique, since the attacker is going to be all over you and in as close as possible. Even after a woman has learned self-defense and knows that she should fight back, it is still difficult for her to step forward and shove her fingers into someone's eyes. Most women wait until the person has grabbed them before taking the attack seriously.

If the thrust gains its power from the body weight and muscle tension, and the snap gains its power from the speed and recoil, where does the scratch get its power? You don't have the room to step in or even the room to snap out and back, so the power comes from side to side. Remember to administer repeated blows from alternating hands. This strike should be practiced in a one-two-three combination--right, left, right.

Let's say the assailant has you up against a wall with both of your hands raised above your head, secured by one of his hands. Eventually, he will have to let go of your hands. He will not be able to rape you while holding your hands up in the air. As soon as he lets go of one or both of your hands, you can begin to ***rip your fingers down into his face***. (see Figure 6)

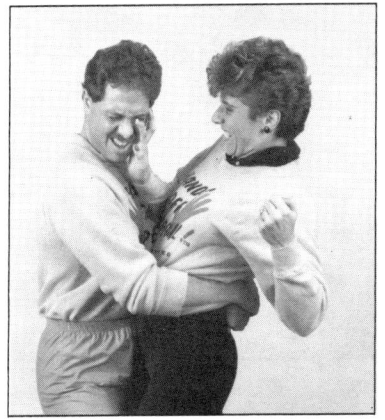

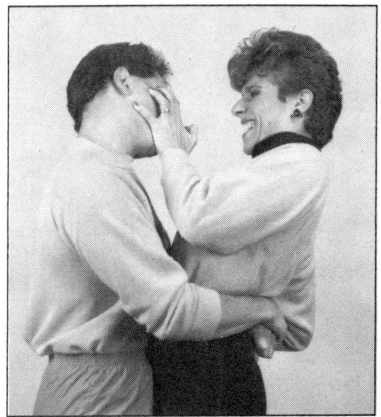

Figure 4

Figure 5

This same variation of the scratch works if the attacker has you pinned down on the ground, again with both hands over your head. (see Figure 6) You could try squirming away from him, but you don't have any leverage from that position. You could try kneeing him in the groin. If that isn't possible, wait until he lets go of one or both of your hands, and then start ripping down into his face.

If someone grabs you by the waist, it is ineffective to push at his shoulders, the way most people naturally would. Not only would your pelvic area be thrust forward into his groin area, you would also experience excruciating pain to your back. He would still probably be able to maintain his grip, and he might enjoy the struggle. In order to get him to let go, shove both of your hands into his face, and *push his head backwards*. This technique will cause the attacker to loosen his grip, but will not immobilize him. For this reason, it is a good technique to use against someone you know and do not wish to cause serious bodily harm. If you are in a life-threatening situation, put the fingers of both hands into his eyes, not just his face. (see Figure 7)

If grabbed from in-close over the arms, you will be unable to strike into the eyes. You may be pulled in too close to knee into the groin. It will then be necessary to *attack the groin with your hand*. Grab hold of the attacker's testicles, and *squeeze* as hard as you can. (see Figure 8) If you cannot manage a tight squeeze (maybe

Figure 6

his pants are too tight), tighten up the palm of your hand, and *slap* or *punch* as hard as you can into the groin. As he is doubling over, push him away from you while yelling "NO!"

The groin grab is also effective if you are sitting or lying down. Often the rapist will require the woman to touch his genitals. This is the perfect opportunity to employ this very effective technique.

If the attacker grabs you from the rear over the arms, chances are that he will not grab you below your elbows. You will still be able to swing your lower arm. Shift your hip to either side, reach

Figure 7

Figure 8

Self-Defense Techniques

Figure 9

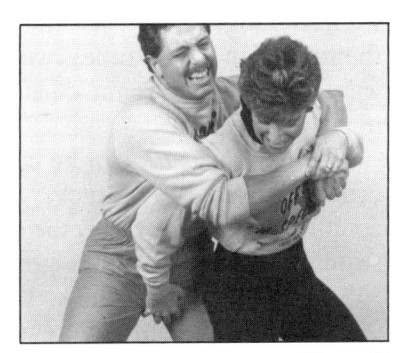

Figure 10

back, and grab the testicles. (see Figure 9) Or you could shift your hip, tighten your fist, and swing it back into the groin as hard as possible. (see Figure 10)

If you are attacked from the rear and you are able to move your elbow, shift the hip to either side, make a fist to tighten your forearm and elbow, and throw the ***elbow back into the assailant's solar plexus*** as hard as you can. (see Figure 11) This will usually make him release his grip, but it will probably not incapacitate him. It will, however, allow some distance between the two of you, and you may be able to escape or execute another self-defense technique. This technique is good to use on someone who is not putting you in a life-threatening situation. Many of the students

Figure 12

Figure 11

we have taught have used the elbow back to the solar plexus on their boyfriends or brothers who were just "goofing around." They wanted the man to remove his hands, but they didn't want to hurt him seriously.

The **elbow back** can be **combined with the fist to the groin** in order to disable the attacker. When grabbed from behind, you could shift your hip, throw the elbow back to the solar plexus, then swing your fist down to the groin.

Now we come to the kicks.

If you have only one choice, which would you rather do-- strike an attacker with your hand into his eyes, or kick to his groin? The answer we most often receive is: kick to his groin. It could be that women are squeamish about drawing blood or witnessing the damage to the attacker's eyes. Another reason is that the notion of retaliating by kicking to the groin has been instilled in females from an early age. Almost every mother has said to her little girl, "Now, sweetie, if any boy ever bothers you, and he won't stop when you ask him, you give him *one swift kick where it counts!*" As a young girl, you might not have known what she meant by that, but the first time you saw a boy doubled over in pain after being hit or kicked in the groin, you quickly understood.

Any time you strike or kick below the belt, the person's body movement or reaction will be to fall over towards you. You now have to push the person away or get out of the way quickly. Whenever you strike or kick above the belt, the person's body will tend to move backwards away from you. This is why we strongly urge self-defense participants to use hand strikes which are performed above the belt, rather than kicks, which are usually delivered below the belt. We don't mean to say that kicks don't work. If done properly, kicks can administer enough pain to the assailant so that you can achieve your goal, which is to escape.

To have the maximum effect, you would want to combine your kick with a hand strike. Whenever you are about to kick, your hands should be up and ready to push the person away or to strike into the face. (see Figure 12)

We call the kick to the groin a *kick and recoil*. In order to inflict damage to the groin area, you must place your foot up and under the testicles and lift the groin area. You must first aim your foot at the groin in order to hit it. Make sure you have proper balance, raise the knee, turn your toes down so you can hit with the instep of your foot, extend your leg, and then bury your foot between his legs so hard that he sees stars! Your foot should be practically sticking out the other end. Never kick for the outside surface area of the groin only. This can very easily be blocked, or you might simply miss by sliding your foot up along his zipper. (see Figure 13) Then the attacker could grab your foot and fling you down onto the ground.

Figure 13

The assailant is not going to stand with his legs apart, waiting for you to kick him in the groin. Unless you have a clear shot at the groin, do not kick. The kick and recoil is done from a distance of one-step-away because you need room to extend your leg.

The tricky part now is to recoil your foot and get it out of there quickly, because if you don't, he could fall on top of you.

The kick that is used from the in-close position is the ***knee into the groin.*** In order for the knee kick to be effective, you must place your *lower thigh*, not your kneecap, directly in between the attacker's legs, and ram it up into the groin as high as possible. (see Figure 14) The higher you raise your knee, the more damage you will do to the groin. To insure that the knee to the groin will be effective, grab the attacker by the sides of the waist, by the shoulders, or by the head, and pull his upper body in towards you. Then drive your lower thigh into the groin as hard as possible. The

60 SEXUAL ASSAULT

Figure 14

Figure 15

Figure 16

Figure 17

Self-Defense Techniques

force and momentum from your pull forward, combined with the thrusting power of your knee driving upwards, will cause excruciating pain to the attacker.

You will not be able to knee into the groin if the person is too close (see Figure 15) because you will not be able to lift your knee.

The knee into the groin can also work if the man is on top of you. Remember, this motion will cause the attacker to fall onto you. It is important to push him away after you complete the technique.

Another kick is the rear snap kick to the groin. If you have been grabbed from behind, quickly snap your heel back into the assailant's groin. (see Figure 16) When your kick connects, the attacker will most certainly fall forwards onto you, so plan to get out of the way. If he does fall on top of you, causing you to fall also, simply get up and run away. He may not be able to get up.

If the attacker is a half-a-step-away, you can kick to the shin. The shin is located above the ankle and below the knee. This is a very effective kick, as it can be done from various positions, it re-

Figure 18   **Figure 19**

Figure 20

Figure 21

quires little training, and it really hurts! Have you ever hit your shin on an end table? Well, imagine the effect you could have by pulling your leg back and then kicking into your attacker's shin as hard as possible. (see Figure 17)

It will hurt him enough to cause him to let go of you and give you time to run. The kick will only temporarily disable him, however. You must run away as quickly as you can, or he may be able to chase you, although he'll probably be limping.

This kick works if the assailant grabs you by the breasts. (You don't think he will? Actually, he is quite likely to grab you by the breasts to shock you.) Don't fight with him by trying to pull his hands off. That's what he wants and expects. Just swing your leg back, and kick him in the shin while yelling, "NO!"

If you are attacked from the rear, you can pull your leg forward and swing the heel of your shoe backwards into his shin. (see Figure 18)

A kick that will decrease the attacker's running ability is called the scrape down the shin. Take the knife edge of your shoe and, starting at the assailant's knee, scrape all the way down the

Self-Defense Techniques

Figure 22

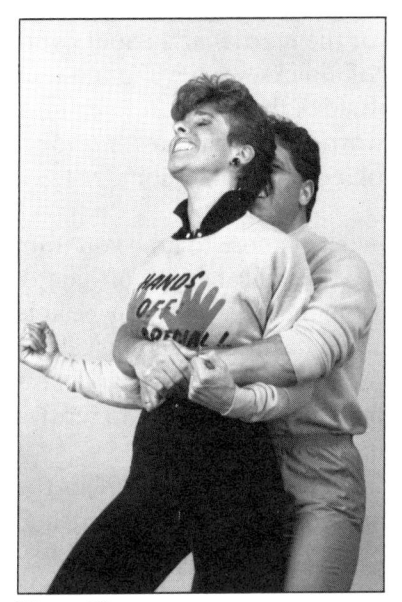

Figure 23

shin; then slam your foot down onto his instep. (see Figures 19 and 20)

If you feel you can't accomplish both of those steps, simply slam your foot down onto the instep very quickly and with as much force as possible.

If attacked from behind and picked up into the air, throw both of your heels back into the attacker, kicking whatever happens to be there. Try to aim for the shin or groin. (see Figure 21) If you are grabbed from the rear and cannot use your hands in any way, or if the assailant has lifted you off the ground, and kicking doesn't seem possible, you can throw your head back into his face as hard as possible. (see Figure 22) This technique is called a head butt, and it will certainly take him by surprise, especially if you accompany it with a loud yell.

The head butt can also be applied during an in-close frontal attack. Simply ram your forehead into his face. (see Figure 23) Yes, you might hurt your head or get a headache. But if it stops the attack, the headache is worth having.

A woman should prepare herself for any type of attack.

When teaching students of karate or the martial arts about overcoming fear of the different kinds of attacks, we have found that practically every novice student is afraid of the attack from behind. We don't want you to become so worried about protecting yourself that you end up constantly looking over your shoulder for a possible attacker.

Think about why an assailant would choose to grab you from behind. Obviously, he wants to scare you and catch you off-guard. He realizes that if he comes at you from the front, you may be able to defend yourself. Already, you have a distinct psychological advantage over him. He has a lack of confidence in himself. That is why he chooses to come at you from behind. A simple defensive move from you could overcome him immediately.

If you are ever attacked from the rear, try to remember the assailant's lack of confidence. Turn your fear into anger, and retaliate with the strongest, loudest yell accompanied by a self-defense technique. Your offensive counter-attack will almost certainly prevent completion of the assault.

The same principle applies in a gang situation. The mentality of the attackers is this: "I can't handle the situation alone. I need the mental and physical support of the others to pull off this attack." Remember, you have the mental advantage. If you can incapacitate one of the attackers, preferably the leader, you can diffuse the "gang" mentality.

If you are confronted with two or more attackers, and you choose to fight back, strike the first one (again, preferably the leader) into the eyes as hard as you possibly can, and begin yelling like a maniac. You might just scare the rest of them away. If the others still proceed to attack, you can attempt the same technique on them or incorporate other self-defense techniques as appropriate.

Try to remember, there is a lot of fear present in the attacker, especially in one who attacks from the rear or with a group. You can intensify the attacker's fear by becoming offensive, and then you can truly turn the situation around.

A student of ours came to us one day and said that she had

tried a particular self-defense technique (the kick to the shin), and it didn't work. Of course, we questioned her further on this.

"I told my boyfriend I was taking this class, and he wanted me to show him what I learned. So he grabbed me from behind, and I did the kick to the shin. And it didn't work."

Marie asked, "Why didn't it work? Did you kick him hard?"

She said, "Well, no, I didn't want to hurt him."

You cannot practice self-defense techniques on people unless you are willing to hurt them. Let's say your boyfriend wants to see how the kick in the groin works. Unless you bury your foot so hard between his legs that he can't get up, he's going to say that the kick didn't work. It makes no sense to demonstrate the techniques to others without using the proper force and execution.

The point we're trying to make is: Don't fool around with self-defense. Save it for a situation in which you feel threatened, and then deliver your counter-attack with everything you've got.

Chapter 7

Conditioning Exercises

One of the most important self-defense techniques is running away. Your self-defense is only as good as your ability to escape the scene. You have to be in good physical condition in order to run what may be quite some distance to get help. That is why we place a heavy emphasis on getting in shape. In addition to the benefit of aiding in your escape, being in good physical shape will make you appear stronger, more confident, and less vulnerable – thus you would be less likely to be targeted for an attack in the first place.

It's easy to find excuses for not being able to defend yourself. "I have weak arms." "I can't run very far." "I'm too small." You are not going to get any sympathy from us. There is always something you can do to improve your fitness level and ability to defend yourself. Do you think your attacker is going to give you any sympathy? Of course, not. If anything, he might choose you because you do have some kind of "handicap" or vulnerable quality. Your mental handicap is probably more limiting than any physical handicap you might have.

We want to start you on your way to becoming a POWER PERSON. We will offer some exercises to increase your flexibility and your muscle strength. These exercises do not form a complete routine, but they will improve your ability to perform the self-defense techniques we have taught you. They should be supplemented by a well-rounded workout program.

Decide now that you want to become a stronger, more capable person—that you want to improve your body structure and your personal appearance—that you want to be the kind of person who can handle any situation. Do this for yourself, in complete selfishness.

Flexibility exercises

Loosen up your neck muscles by performing neck rolls. Standing with legs one-shoulder-length apart and arms at your sides, rotate your head first to the left side 10 times, and then to the right 10 times. (see Figure 24)

Next, perform the waist twist. Face forward in the same position as before. Raise your elbows to shoulder level, and twist the upper half of your body from side to side. (see

Figure 24

Figure 25

Figure 25) Do this 15 times.

To stretch your hamstring (back of thigh), sit on the floor with your legs straight in front of you, bend at the waist, and stretch your upper body over your legs and down as far as you can. Try to touch your nose to your knee. Do this hamstring stretch in a continuous stretching motion; don't bounce up and down. Hold for a count of eight. Do five stretches on each leg.

Figure 26

Another exercise to stretch the hamstring as well as the lower back is performed while standing. Cross one foot over another and stretch down, trying to touch your palms to the floor. (see Figure 26) Hold this position for five seconds. Do five stretches on each leg.

To improve flexibility throughout your inner thigh and hip area, start from the position described above, but stretch only one leg out as far as you can. Bend the other leg at the knee, touching your heel to your buttocks. This is called a hurdler's stretch. Now, reaching towards the outstretched leg, bend down and try to touch your nose to your knee. Hold that position for a count of eight, repeating five times. Switch to the opposite side.

To strengthen and stretch the front of the thigh (the quadricep muscles), try doing the hinge. Kneel down and sit on your heels. Point your toes. With knees together and your back absolutely straight, slowly lower your upper body as far back as possible. (see Figure

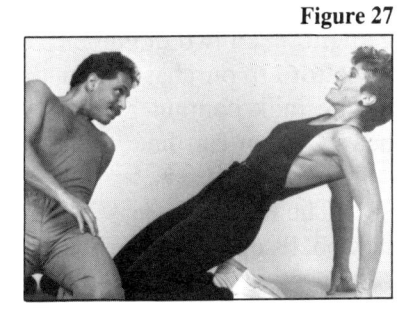

Figure 27

Figure 28  **Figure 29**

27) You will feel the stretch along the front of the thigh.

Another front thigh stretch is performed by standing erect and grabbing the toe of the foot, pulling it back and up towards the buttocks. (see Figure 28) Do five of these with each leg.

Now that your muscles are warmed up, perform 50 jumping jacks. Do these standing straight and tall, straddling your legs as far apart as you can on the down beat, and clapping your hands over your head on the up beat. (see Figure 29)

Muscle development exercises

In order to develop your muscles, you must use weight resistance. Don't worry about becoming "too muscular." In order for the average woman to acquire bulging muscles, she would have to spend many hours doing progressive weight training. What we are advocating here is only a small amount of weight training for the purpose of gaining muscle strength.

Let's start by working on the arms and upper body. You are going to need two dumbbells, about six pounds each. If you cannot afford to purchase them, then use water to fill two one-gallon plastic milk containers that have handles. Make them only as heavy as you can handle easily at first, gradually increasing the weight.

The first exercise is called the shoulder roll. Stand erect, with dumbbells down at your sides. Roll your shoulders backwards 10

Figure 30

Figure 31

times; then rest, and roll them forwards 10 times. (see Figures 30 and 31)

Next, perform the alternating bicep curl. Stand erect with your feet about a half-a-shoulder-length apart, slightly bending your knees. Hold a dumbbell in each hand, with your arms down at your sides, palms facing forward. Lift the dumbbell in your right hand until it almost touches your chest. Now as you slowly lower the dumbbell to the original position, have the left arm perform the same movement. (see Figure 32) Do 10 repetitions on each side; rest for a minute; then do another set of 10 each. This exercise will greatly improve your ability to perform the thrusting technique into the eyes.

To strengthen the shoulders and arms, try the alternating over-head dumbbell press. Begin by standing erect with your feet a half-a-shoulder-length apart. Holding the dumbbells in your hands, raise them up to shoulder level with your elbows tucked in, palms facing in towards your face. Raise your right arm over your head, controlling the weight the entire time. As you bring your arm down to the original starting position, begin to raise the other arm. (see Figure 33) Do 10 repetitions with each arm. Rest for one minute; then do another set of 10 each.

Next, try the shoulder strengthener. Start with the weights down at your sides. Slowly raise them laterally to a height above your head. Do 20 of these.

To strengthen the muscles on the back of your upper arm

Figure 32

Figure 33

(the triceps), perform the tricep extension. Hold a dumbbell over your head with one or both hands. Bending at the elbow, slowly lower the dumbbell behind your head, then return it to the starting position. (see Figure 34) Do 10 of these. Rest, then do 10 more.

The lunge will strengthen your thighs and make your kicks more powerful. Stand erect with your feet less than a half-a-shoulder-length apart. Hold the dumbbells down by your side, arms completely extended. Begin by stepping forward about three feet with your right leg. Slowly bend it so that you cannot see your toes. Your left leg should be bent and touching the floor now. (see Figure 35) Keep your back erect. You should feel the stress in the front of your thigh and in your buttocks. Hold this position for two seconds. Now push off of your right leg, and return to the original position. Repeat with the other leg. Alternate legs, performing 10 lunges with each leg.

Figure 34

Another good thigh-strengthening exercise is the deep knee bend. Start with your feet about one-shoulder-length apart, toes pointed out in front. Holding a dumbbell in each hand, bend your arms at the el-

Figure 35

Figure 36

Figure 37

bows. Now squat down until your thighs are parallel with the floor. (see Figure 36) Do this exercise 20 times. If your knees are weak, try turning your toes slightly outwards while performing the exercise. It is normal for the knees to make a cracking sound.

An exercise that can strengthen your legs and increase your heart rate, is the step-up. You will need a large wooden or concrete block that will support your weight. Hold a dumbbell in each hand. Using your right leg, step up on and then down off the block, using your left leg to support your body. (see Figure 37) Alternate legs, stepping up 20 times with each leg. The faster you perform this routine, the more you will increase your heart rate.

To perform the calf stretch, stand on a board or stair. Holding the dumbbells down by your sides, push your body up so that you are standing on the balls of your feet. (see Figure 38) Feel the stretch and pull in your calf muscles. Do this exercise 20 times.

Exercises to do with a partner

If you have a husband or partner, you may want to include

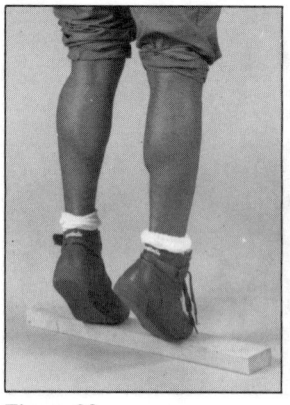

Figure 38

Figure 39

him in your exercise regimen. He can improve his fitness level, and the two of you can have fun at the same time. Set your routine to music, and it will be even more enjoyable.

First of all, you can do your stretches together. Start with the waist stretch. Both of you should sit on the floor with your legs straddled (out to the sides) as far as possible. Face each other with your feet touching. Grasp his left wrist with your left hand, and have him do the same to you. Raise your right arm over your head, and stretch down to your left side. Try to touch your left foot with your right hand. As you are doing this, your partner is adding resistance by doing the same thing. (see Figure 39) Stretch 12 times to the left side. Reverse the position and stretch 12 times to the right. This exercise stretches the obliques (sides of waist), buttocks, hamstring, and inner thigh muscles.

Another good limbering exercise is called rowboats. Remain in the straddled position. Grab a firm hold of your partner's opposite wrists. (Your right hand grabs his left wrist; your left hand grabs his right wrist.) You slowly bend your body to the right side, rolling all the way back

Figure 40

and then around to your left side. All the while, your partner is stretching with you. (see Figures 40) As you return to the starting position, he now rolls back and around, and you stretch with him. This exercise strengthens and tones the lower back, buttocks, and hamstring muscles.

Figure 41

Sit-ups will strengthen and build the abdominals. Strong stomach muscles will give power to your strikes and enable you to lift your legs with enough force to perform the kicks. Lie on your back with your knees up, feet flat on the floor. Have your partner do the same thing, with his feet intertwining with yours. Place your hands behind your neck. Now tighten your abdominals, and raise your upper body so that your chest touches your knees. (see Figure 41) Be careful not to pull on your neck muscles to lift you up. Slowly lower yourself and repeat the movement at least 10 times at first, gradually increasing the repetitions.

Push-ups will build and strengthen your upper body. Lie face down on the ground, with palms on the floor right beside your face. Now straighten your arms, and lift your entire chest off the floor. If you are weak in the shoulders and arms, then do bent-knee push-ups. Perform the push-ups as described, but with your knees bent so that your legs form a 45-degree angle. (see Figure 42) Do as many push-ups as you can. As you progress, you can have your partner apply some weight resistance by pushing on your back while you lift up. Your mate's upper body may be stronger

Figure 42

Figure 43

Figure 44

Figure 45

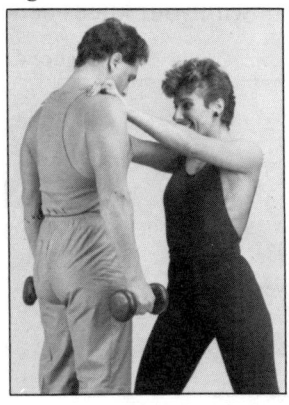

Figure 46

than yours. If he can do push-ups with ease, then you can sit on his back as he performs the exercise. (see Figure 43)

To strengthen your biceps, triceps, and shoulder muscles, try the pull-up. Have your partner stand directly in front of you. Place your feet about a half-a-shoulder-length apart, keeping your elbows close to your side. Bend your arms with your palms facing up, at about waist level. Have him place his palms face down on top of your palms. As you lift your palms, have him press down, adding resistance. (see Figure 44) When your hands reach breast level, return them to the original position. Repeat 15 times. Your partner can apply as much pressure as you wish, gradually increasing over time.

The opposite of the pull-up is the push-down. Begin with your feet in the original position. This time, raise your hands to breast level, palms facing down. Tucking your elbows in, have your partner grasp your hands with his palms facing up. As you push down, your mate adds resistance by trying to force your hands back up. (see Figure 45) Keep pushing down until you reach waist level. Perform 15 repetitions. You can vary the movement by pointing your elbows outwards to exercise the pectoral (breast) muscles.

Instead of using dumbbells on your calf raises, you can have your partner provide weight resistance for you. Stand straight, feet together, arms at the side. Have

Figure 47

your partner stand behind you with his hands on your shoulders. Have him push down as you lift your heels off the floor, raising them as high as you can, then lowering them. (See Figure 46) Repeat 25 times.

Try performing the step-up exercise with your partner. Stand facing each other, with the block on the floor between you. Holding hands, take turns stepping up onto the block. (see Figure 47) Do 50 step-ups.

To strengthen your calves, thighs, buttocks, and abdominals, try the leg press. Lie on your back with your knees bent towards your chest, and the heels of your feet pushed out. Have your partner rest his lower abdomen against your feet. He will be supported by your feet, leaning over the top of you. Grab each other's hands and try to balance him on your feet. Straighten your feet, and raise him up as high as you can while still keeping your balance. Be careful to prevent him from falling over on top of you. See how many times you can press his weight. You'll have lots of fun trying to do this one.

Practicing self-defense techniques

The best way to be prepared to perform self-defense techniques is to practice the maneuvers. Give yourself plenty of room, and try to work in front of a mirror so you can watch yourself and chart your progress.

First practice the thrust into the eyes. Stand with your feet one-shoulder-length apart, hands at your side. Step forward one large step with your right leg, thrusting your weight forward while tightening up your hand and striking into the air at your own eye level. Do this 15 times with each hand. Remember to always step in with a hand and leg from the same side. Yell "NO!" as you thrust. The constant contraction of the hand and leg will strengthen your arm and leg muscles.

Now stand with your feet one-shoulder-length or less apart. You're going to practice the snap and recoil, which requires speed. Take a short step, and snap your hand out and back as quickly as you can. Remember to tighten up your hand, but recoil it back quickly. Practice for your own eye level, and remember to yell. Do this 15 times on each side.

If you want to connect with something during your hand strikes, have your partner hold a thick pillow up at his head level with his arms outstretched. Step forward, and thrust your hands into the pillow.

Practice the knee into the groin by starting with your feet almost a shoulder-length apart. Move your right leg back about half-a-shoulder-length. Hold your hands in front of you, elbows tucked in to protect your upper body. Whenever you practice the kicking techniques, always have your hands up and ready to strike, grab, or push away. Now tighten up your right leg, tuck your heel up so it almost touches your buttocks, and drive your knee forward and as high up as possible. Do this 10 times with each leg. Rest one minute, then do 10 more with each leg.

To practice the kick into the shin, start by moving your right leg one-shoulder-length wide and one-shoulder-length back. Keep the hands up in a ready position, and bring the leg forward by snapping out at the knee quickly, out and back. Make sure that you look down as if you were looking at someone's shin. When you practice this kick, pull your toes back, and kick with the ball of your foot. We do not suggest kicking the wall, but if you have a beam or pole in your house, wrap pillows or blankets around it securely, and it will make a good target.

To practice the kick into the groin, begin with your feet parallel to one another. Move your right leg two-shoulder-lengths wide, and two-shoulder-lengths back. Face your hips and your shoulders forward. Keep your rear heel planted down. Have your hands up and ready to block possible strikes or kicks. Bend your rear leg at the knee, turn your toes down, and snap your foot out as if it were penetrating a groin. Recoil it back; then return to the original position. Do this ten times on each side. Rest one minute, and do another set of ten each. If you want to practice this technique with your partner, have him stand in front of you just out of your kicking range. Have him bend over towards you slightly. Practice kicking your foot out and recoiling it as quickly as you can. Have him try to grab your foot. If he is able to grab it, then you are not recoiling quickly enough. Remember, the attacker is not going to be standing over you, ready to grab your foot. So if your mate does grab it a few times, don't be discouraged. Your partner could also hold a pillow parallel with the floor, and you could kick up into it.

Practice running with your partner. Instead of jogging at a slow pace, practice doing wind sprints. Start at a certain point, then bolt away as quickly as possible for at least 20 yards. Then return to the starting point. When your partner says "Go," bolt away again, but this time run 30 yards. Do five sprints, each time increasing the yardage. This is a very tiring activity, but a very beneficial one.

A student of ours enthusiastically told us of her doctor's report describing the pulled muscles in both of her legs. Asking her to explain further, she related a recent attack which ended after she kicked into the assailant's shin. What followed the kick, as she described it, was a "run of terror." She had run, without stopping, six blocks to a friend's house, where she collapsed. Her smiling account of the story only proves that self-defense involves not just striking or kicking, but in her words,"running your rear end off."

End your routine with some neck rolls and light stretching to cool down. Your workout should be done daily to maintain general fitness. Incorporate jogging, bicycling, and aerobics to your activities. Serious weight training is recommended not only to increase your strength, but to keep your body feeling and looking better. Once you see the results of your efforts, you'll want to make sure you don't miss your workouts. Remember, you are doing this for yourself, and you should give it your maximum effort.

Chapter 8

Natural Defenses

If you are chosen as the target of a sexual assault, you will probably ask, "Why me?" This nagging question plagues people who have suffered any kind of tragedy. You could rationalize that you were being punished for a wrongdoing you may have committed in the past, or to find yourself guilty of somehow enticing the rapist. It serves no purpose to try to come up with a reason. And there certainly is no sense in your assuming the blame for a crime committed against you.

Chances are that you became a rape victim because you exhibited some of the three elements of availability, accessibility, and vulnerability.

Availability — you happened to be in the wrong place at the wrong time.

Accessibility — the rapist considered you approachable, easily attainable.

Vulnerability — you appeared weak, defenseless, fearful, lost, depressed, under the influence of drugs or alcohol, unaware, or too trusting.

Rape is not inevitable. Rape can be avoided. Your state of mind, the attitude you exude, and the behaviors you exhibit can be the determining factors of whether or not you will be deemed a good target. Eliminate the three qualities listed above, and you will lessen your chances of becoming a victim.

Your natural defenses

We are all born with natural defenses or instincts. We are talking about the natural impulses or actions that are essential to our well-being or preservation. In our civilized society, we have been taught to set aside many of our natural instincts. If people are cautious, they're labeled paranoid. If they retaliate after an attack, they're called barbarians. We think this is nonsense. We must train ourselves to recognize our natural defenses and redevelop them.

Awareness — Be aware of things around you. Look around, noticing as much as you can about your surroundings. Don't walk around in a daze with your head in the clouds. Criminals can sense uncertainty or lack of awareness.

Precaution — Always expect the unexpected. Plan your use of time. Be in charge of your whereabouts and activities. Don't sit back and let others decide things for you. When you sense danger, take a preventive measure to avoid it. Don't tell yourself that you are being paranoid. If you think someone is following you, turn around and look! If your suspicions are correct, start running. If you think something is wrong, or you feel uncomfortable in a situation, you're probably right. Don't hesitate to correct the situation or get yourself out of it. Remember, your safety is most important. This is not the time to consider the other person's feelings.

Don't worry that you might look silly. It's not silly to avoid a potential attack. It is silly to wait for the attack to begin before you take action.

Involvement — If something does happen, involve yourself! Don't crawl up in a ball of fear and ask yourself, "Why is this happening to me?" Understand that it is, and try to do something about it. Turn your fear into anger. If you're angry, you will tend to do more to defend yourself.

Developing your natural defenses

When a baby is born, it exhibits its natural defenses often. As the young child grows, its parents have to foster a continued reliance on natural defenses. It may have seemed to you as a teenager that you never had any freedom. You may have resented the fact that your older siblings could do things you weren't allowed to do. Think about how you might have acted as a young teen:

    Mom: "Where are you going?"
    Teen: "Out."
    Mom: "Out, where?"
    Teen: "Around."
    Mom: "Around where?"
    Teen: "You know, around with my friends."
    Mom: "What friends?"
    Teen: "A few guys, a few girls."
    Mom: "How are you getting there?"
    Teen: "Oh, I don't know. Maybe we'll walk; maybe we'll get a ride."
    Mom: "When will you be home?"
    Teen: "I don't know—in a little while."

This teen hasn't learned how to handle independence. Her parents are not confident that she is able to take care of herself. They are probably right.

At some point, (we hope) the teen matures. The parents can see competent, responsible behavior, and they feel reasonably assured that the young adult is capable of handling more freedom. This is how a conversation might go:

    Mom: "Where are you going?"
    Teen: "Well, I'm going over to Mary's house for about an hour; then we're both going to pick up Sue and go to McDonald's for a bite to eat."
    Mom: "Okay. What time are you coming home?"
    Teen: "I'll be home by 9:30. If something comes up to delay me, I'll call you."
    Mom: "Good. How are you getting there?"
    Teen: "Well, Mom, I was hoping you'd drive me. Would that be all right?"
    Mom: "Yes, I can give you a ride. Are you ready to go now?"

This teen showed a great deal of maturity—having carefully planned and organized the evening out and having shared the "specifics" of this information with the parent. She is decreasing the chances of appearing available, accessible, or vulnerable to a potential attacker. The three natural defenses—awareness, precaution, and involvement—are all highly developed and at the teen's disposal. She would not be a good target for assault.

Chapter 9

I Need Answers

1. How would I recognize a physical assault?

A physical assault begins with a forward movement from one-step-away or less. If a visual or verbal assault has taken place, and now the person is moving towards you, it is time to react. Do something. Back up, run, yell, strike, or kick. But always try to keep that one-step-away distance so you can escape.

2. What should I do if the attacker has a weapon?

Do whatever he wants you to do until you can safely react. Gain his confidence. Make him feel as though he can trust you, and he may lower or put down the weapon.

Leading him on may be your best course of action. He may believe you are submitting and will not try to escape. As soon as you see him relax his grip on you, you can try some positive action like striking, kicking, or running. But don't kid yourself and think that you can dodge bullets or kick a knife out of his hand.

Remember, if he becomes violent immediately, and you believe that he will not hesitate to use the weapon, submitting may be your best choice. The decision is yours. You can recover from rape with proper counseling. It's better to be alive to deal with the problem than to be dead.

3. If I submit, will that stop the rape?

In some situations, submitting may stop the physical beating.

The rapist would probably prefer the struggle to the submission, but chances are, however, that the sexual assault will continue.

4. Will crying or begging work to stop the rape?

There is a slight possibility that this course of action will appeal to an attacker's sympathetic side and he will stop the rape, particularly if the assailant is an acquaintance of yours. In most cases, however, it will have either of the following undesired outcomes. It will excite the man to greater proportions, giving him the feeling he is trying to achieve--that he has humiliated and degraded you. Or, it may make him angrier and cause him to be more violent in his physical assault.

Crying and begging are negative responses. We believe in positive action. But, again, any action is better than none at all. You are the one who has to assess the situation and decide which action to take.

5. When should I use passive resistance?

Through our years of teaching, we have learned that most women have little or no fighting experience. Unless you are going to fight with all the force you can possibly muster, then you should not fight at all. Passive resistance is the choice that comes most naturally to many women. Of course, it only works if the attacker is willing to listen to you. It is probably most effective if you are acquainted with him, and you think he will listen to reason.

6. Should I yell or scream?

A scream is a sound that you make when you are scared. A yell, on the other hand, is a sound that you make when you are angry. Yelling will help you turn your fear into anger. Yell whatever it takes to help you get angry. We suggest the word, "NO!" Practice yelling "NO" while stepping forward with an open hand strike into the air.

7. When should I fight back?

The decision is yours, but fight back as soon as you possibly can. The longer you wait, the harder it will be to defend against a physical attack. The odds are against the victim as the attack goes on, but even if a good deal of time has elapsed, when you see an opportunity to fight, you should take it.

Remember, self-defense works only if you strike or kick to vital areas. Use every ounce of speed and power you can muster. Give the attacker NO MERCY. Then, run! Keep in mind that your only goal is to escape, not to fight punch for punch.

8. It is ever too late to fight back?

That decision is totally up to you. It is never too late to change a decision in favor of submitting to one of fighting back. Let's say you have been submissive and now are being penetrated. At this point, the rapist's defenses will be down. He doesn't expect you to fight back. Surprise him! Shove all of your fingers into his face, or squeeze his genitals forcefully.

Most rapists will force a woman to perform oral copulation. If anything comes near your mouth, bite and bite hard! Follow up any of these techniques with a strong run.

9. If I fight back, won't the attacker just become angrier?

Let's face it, if you hit a man in the eyes or groin, he will become angry. You have to count on the element of surprise. The attacker does not expect a strong, violent defense from his victim. After you strike, don't wait around to see how he is--RUN!

10. What if he is too big or too tall?

If you are attacked by a large man, you still have your three choices. If you submit, the attack may be more brutal because of his size alone. Talking your way out may work. Fighting back is not out of the question because he still has vulnerable spots--eyes, groin, and shin. You must hit or kick harder, and run faster, but remember to do your best and give one hundred percent. Show NO MERCY!

11. What if there is more than one attacker?

Your choices are still the same. If you submit, then all of them will take turns sexually assaulting you, each one trying to outdo the other. We suggest you try talking to or attacking the leader. If he backs down, the others will follow.

Especially in this situation, an ounce of prevention is worth a pound of cure. If you spot a group of unsavory characters, change your direction or get out of their way, even if doing so takes you out of your way.

12. What if the attacker is someone I know--should I really try to hurt him?
This is the hardest point to bring across to women. You cannot worry about hurting the man. You've got to understand that he wants to force sexual intercourse against your will. He is not worried about how it's going to affect you.

13. How should I handle a flasher?
A flasher is someone who has had little or no sexual experience. He is afraid of a normal one-to-one intimacy with a woman. Yet many men escalate from flashers to rapists. Do not take this type of attack lightheartedly. Do not believe the myth that flashers will never attack you physically. Be cautious, and expect the unexpected. If you are the victim of a flasher, the best thing you can do is try not to have any reaction at all. Do not scream or laugh at the flasher. Leave the location quickly. Report the incident to the police, and give a description of the man and the time and location of the event.

14. How do I handle an obscene phone call?
Hang up.
But, what if the caller persists?
HANG UP. HANG UP. HANG UP! Do not talk to the caller, or try to figure out who he is. Do not scream at him, or call him a disgusting pig. Any remarks to the person, whether negative or otherwise, will encourage him to make repeat calls. If you keep hanging up, the caller will get tired of hearing a dial tone and will call some other unfortunate person. Report these calls to the police.

15. How should I handle guys who touch me when they talk to me?
Why do women allow this to go on without saying something to the man? If you are with a man, and he touches you in a way that makes you uncomfortable, take his hand off of you! You don't

have to hit it or slap it away, causing a confrontation. If necessary, simply state to him that you want him to remove his hand. Stop the problem at the onset. If you allow it to continue, it will. Remember our motto: "Hands Off: I'm Special!"

16. How do I handle a visual attack?

If someone is staring at you, by no means turn around or totally ignore him. Doing so would be putting yourself in a position to be attacked from the rear. Do not stare back at the person, but turn slightly so that you can still keep him in view. Make no verbal contact, or you may cause a confrontation. Try to walk away if you can, but be aware of any foreseeable danger.

17. How do I handle a verbal attack?

A verbal attack can be thought of as any remark that is suggestive or demeaning. We feel that the best defense is for you to remain silent. Remember, the reason he made the remark is to make you feel embarassed or uncomfortable. Do not give the man the satisfaction of knowing that his statement had an effect on you. If you do come back with more verbalizations, he has easily manipulated you into conversation, even if it is of a negative nature. You may cause a direct conflict which could lead to a physical attack.

18. What do I do if I am being followed?

Remember, your natural defenses--awareness, precaution, and involvement--are your key assets in preventing an attack. The correct procedure when walking or driving is to take as many precautionary measures as possible.

When walking, always know your route before you go out. Do not walk in search of the correct streets, or look as though you are lost. At the first sign of being followed, take a precautionary measure. Do not panic, but if you decide to increase speed, don't increase a little; increase all the way. In other words, don't walk faster--RUN!

When driving, don't drive all over town in hopes of losing the car that's following you. Don't just drive faster; drive somewhere. Choose an open store, a supermarket, a restaurant, or a police station.

19. What if my car breaks down?

Auto breakdowns precede most sexual attacks that occur on highways. Again, we cannot overemphasize the importance of precaution and prevention. Make sure your car is in good running order, and you have plenty of gas. If the car does break down on a highway, you should raise the hood, get in the car, close the windows, and lock the doors. If someone stops to help, ask him to call the police. Do not get into a stranger's car.

If your car breaks down on a city street, go to a nearby gas station or an open store. Call someone you know, and give your location. Have your friend pick you up right where you are. Don't worry about your car.

If you have no one to call, then call the police.

20. What about hitchhiking?

DON'T! Never hitchhike, or pick up hitchhikers--either male or female.

We have heard girls ask, "But what if I have to hitchhike, then what?"

We feel there should be no reason whatsoever for you to get yourself into an easy trouble situation such as hitchhiking. If you feel there is no other choice but to hitchhike, ask the driver his or her destination before entering the car. If you are answered with an unsure location or a vague response (such as, "Why, you want me to take you any place special?"), don't get in. Wait for another car. Do not enter a car after the driver has slammed on his brakes or changed his direction to pick you up.

If you do enter a car, check the locks and the handles on the door. Check the interior of the car for unusual objects or other clues to a possible trouble situation. Don't worry about insulting the driver. If the person does not have anything unsavory in mind, he or she will respect your precaution.

21. What should I do if I'm out on a date or with friends, and I'm left stranded?

Don't make it possible for you to be left stranded without means of returning home. Always carry enough money to pay for cabfare. If you have no money, find a place where you can use a phone, and call a friend or family member for help.

22. A male friend has asked me out, but he won't take no for an answer. His persistence is starting to scare me. What should I do?
Try not to play the silly communication games that men and women play in the dating situation. An honest, strong-willed explanation of your denial to date him should be enough. If he still persists, consider him like any other threatening person. You should report him or act accordingly.

23. It seems like I always get the date who says I owe him something for the evening out. How do I handle that?
As long as women use sexual activity as a payoff for money spent on them, men will continue to reason that their expectations are appropriate. Be honest and "up front." Explain in advance that you would like to split the cost of the entire evening. Do not agree to a second date with a man who used his expenses as an excuse for his sexual aggressiveness.

24. What if I'm on public transportation, and the person next to me accidentally rubs up against me, or his hand touches my leg, etc.?
First of all, it is no accident. Everyone knows where his hands are, and the man who lays his hand on your leg knows what he's doing. Take his hand off of you, and find a new seat. If you make a scene and humiliate him in front of other people, you may set him off and cause yourself further trouble. Keep an eye on him discreetly to be sure he doesn't get off at your stop and follow you.

25. But what if I do move to another seat, and he follows?
Sit towards the front of the bus, or near a group of people. Talk to the driver or the other people, and explain what has happened. But don't expect others to rescue you from the situation. Be prepared to defend yourself.

26. What if I'm in a movie theater, and a man sits next to me?
You could make a scene. You know how one little sound attracts attention in a theater. The man may become quite embarassed and leave.

The course of action we most prefer is that you relocate. Some women say to this, "But I have just as much of a right to sit there as he does."

We say, "Yes, you do, but don't let your rights interfere with your safety."

If you do move to another seat, and he moves along with you, go to the movie office and give the manager a description of the man. By all means, don't go to the women's washroom, thinking it's the safest place--because it isn't. Just because it says "Women" on the door doesn't mean he won't enter.

Remember, of course, to be on the lookout for the man as you leave the theater later.

27. *What if a male friend of the family comes to the door and asks to come in? I don't want to be rude and turn him away. What should I do?*

Many women have allowed themselves to be put in a position to be attacked because they didn't want to be rude to an acquaintance. Be cautious any time you are home alone. In the long run, you will gain more respect than ridicule. Always think of yourself, because that's exactly what the man is doing.

28. *Should I carry a weapon?*

Psychologists have found that people rely on weapons for a false sense of confidence. Unless they have used the weapon on a regular basis, they are not likely to use it effectively in a high-pressure situation or surprise attack. They usually freeze, or go into temporary shock.

A weapon is only an extension of your fighting ability. If you do not have confidence in your own self-defense capabilities, carrying a weapon will serve no purpose whatsoever. Any weapon that you carry can be taken away and used against you. Do not trust your safety to a weapon.

Your natural defenses--awareness, precaution, and involvement--are your best weapons.

29. *Is chemical Mace a deterrent against rape?*

Mace is a chemical that works on the central nervous system and mucous membrane. When sprayed directly into a person's eyes or nose, it is designed to cause tears, dizziness, immobilization, and sometimes nausea. Be wary if a salesman claims that Mace will enable you to stop a charging attacker in his tracks.

We don't want you to trust your safety to any product. First of all, you'd have to be carrying it at all times, and have it quickly at your disposal, which is unlikely during a surprise attack. Secondly, the attacker has to be coming at you from the front, and you have to have a good shot at his face in order for it to be effective.

What we hear is, "But it sprays up to 15 feet away. That way, I don't have to get close to him if he attacks."

Our answer to that is that if you are 15 feet away from your attacker, don't fight. RUN! Remember, you won't recognize an attack until it is at least three steps away, or less.

30. What about putting my keys between my fingers for use as a weapon?

This is not a bad idea, because it makes sense to have your keys in your hand as you are walking home or towards your car so that you are not caught off guard while searching for them. Any weapon that works and can be used easily and effectively is a good addition to your arsenal.

How should you place your keys for use in this manner? Hold the one key you need in the normal manner, and put the rest in a weapon-like position, sticking out from between your other fingers. At the time of an attack, thrust your hand with all your might directly into the assailant's face. Remember, this will work only if you have no second thoughts about hurting your attacker.

Our only problem with this method is that we fear you may rely strictly on the keys, and put all of your confidence into them. What happens, then, if the attacker grabs your hand, causing you to drop the keys? There goes your confidence.

31. The strike to the eyes sounds effective, but what if the attacker is wearing glasses?

This is a question we are frequently asked. It almost seems as if women are ready to find excuses for not defending themselves. The answer to the question is: hit as hard as you can directly into the glasses. Quite possibly, you will break off some of the frame, or the glasses themselves will shatter. Shoving the parts into his eyes will give you time to escape. You cannot worry about the well-being of someone who is threatening you with bodily harm.

32. Can a man be raped?

This question usually brings snickers from members of the audience. Most of them imagine a woman forcing a man to get an erection and then have sex with her. Many men think, "I would love for that to happen."

Others say, "Impossible. How could a woman rape a man?"

There are many situations in which a man could be raped. A gang of angry women could be looking to dominate and humiliate a man. He could be overpowered, tied down, and raped anally by an object.

A single woman could initially seduce the man, who would allow himself to be restrained in some way. Then she might rape him, beat him, and/or castrate him.

A man could be raped by another man. This situation does not necessarily mean that the attacker or the victim is gay. The attacker perceives the male victim as an object for control, domination, and humiliation.

33. What is statutory rape?

Statutory rape occurs when a girl under the legal age of consent agrees to have sexual intercourse with a man over the legal age of consent. The legal age of consent varies from state to state. The most common ages of consent are 16 to 18. Consult your local police for this information.

34. Is it true that women "ask" to be raped?

By its very definition, rape only occurs against one's wishes.

Some people find it easier to blame the woman for the attack. They will reason that since she was dressed provocatively or wore excessive make-up, she was trying to entice all men. Let's turn that situation around.

We ask our audience, "Ladies, if you see a handsome man wearing a nice pair of tight jeans, are you suddenly hit with an uncontrollable urge to run up to him, beat him, sexually assault him, and tell him how much fun he's having? Then, after it's all over, imagine other people saying, 'Well, did you see what he was wearing? He asked for it.'"

To say that the victim "asked for it" is only to give an excuse for an inexcusable crime.

35. What's the first thing I should do after I've been raped?

Immediately get to a hospital, even if you were not beaten. If you call the police, they will take you to the hospital. You may want a friend or family member to accompany you. Do not wash, douche, or bathe. Do not change your clothing. Bring a change of clothes with you, if possible. Your clothes will be taken as evidence.

The following medical procedures should be followed:

a. Blood test--to detect if venereal disease was present in you at the time of the attack, and another test six weeks later to determine if venereal disease was contracted during the attack.

b. Urinalysis--to detect if you were pregnant at the time of the attack, and another test in six weeks to determine if impregnation occurred during the attack.

c. Acid phosphatase and semen smear--to be used as evidence if the assailant is brought to trial.

d. Pelvic examination--to check for internal injuries.

Most importantly, a victim should make arrangements to receive professional counseling.

Chapter 10

Personal Experiences

Therese--Age 16

My experience wasn't anything like Marie went through, but it was still scary to me. It was a weekend night, and I had a few girlfriends over. One of my friends said, "Looks like we have visitors."

I opened the door, and here were three guys. I knew all three, and one of them was my best buddy, I thought. He came in and ran downstairs to the bar. I don't like my friends drinking in my house, because my parents trust me. I ran downstairs after him and tried to get him away from the bar. He pushed me up against the wall and tried to kiss me.

I said, "No!"

He kept on saying, "Yes," and pushing me farther and farther to the wall. I got real scared because he is 6'6" and weighs 225 pounds, and I couldn't get him off. Finally I yelled for my friends, and they got him to leave me alone. Thanks to this class I might be able to do something, because my friends might not be there again.

Shannon -- Age 15

I was going out with this guy for two weeks. One night we were alone at his house, and we started kissing. My boyfriend started to go further than I wanted. He started to go down my pants, and I asked him not to. He got mad and tried again. Then he wanted me to go down his pants. I wouldn't, and he got mad again. He kept asking me why I didn't want to do those things with him. I told him I was scared. He couldn't understand my point of view. He was the first guy I was ever with who tried anything on me. To most girls that wouldn't be any big deal, but it was to me. I really felt bad about it. But after taking your class, it really helped me to understand that he had no right to make me do anything I didn't want to do. I don't think he had any right to get mad at me either. After that night I felt really sick to my stomach. You guys really made me feel better about myself. I talked to my boyfriend about what happened and some of the things you taught me. He's been pretty cool to me lately. He understands more now than he did before. I guess he'll just have to wait until I'm ready. I'm not going to feel bad about myself anymore or do anything I don't want to. If he wants to make me do something I don't want to, then he's not worth it.

Sandi--Age 14

When I was in 8th grade, two older guys, 16 and 17, picked me and two of my friends up from a dance. We went to my neighborhood and over to one of their places. About three other guys were there. I was in the bathroom combing my hair when three or four of them came into the room. They pushed me through the door and onto the bed in the bedroom. They all jumped on top of me. Their hands were all over me. I thought they were just trying to joke around because we were all pretty good friends. I pulled one guy's hair as hard as I could, and he jumped. They all got off me then, and the one guy was really mad at me. I still see all of them a lot because they're always in the neighborhood, but I don't take their crap anymore. After taking your class, I now feel that if I was in that position again, I would know what to do.

Diane--Age 14

When I was in 7th grade, I lived in a small town in

Washington that didn't have many people. I was on the track team with two other girls and 15 guys. Eight were nice, but the other seven were jerks. One day after practice, I came in and these guys, Don and Todd, were in the locker room. They had Kari up in the air screaming at them to put her down. They did, and then left.

The next day she quit track because they had hurt her back. When practice was over, I went into the locker room to change. I heard the door open, and there were about six of the guys coming at me. Don, who was about 6'9", put me up in the air against the wall, and the others guys grabbed me and used fingers in some places. I screamed and kicked and punched. I knocked one of them in the face and kicked one in the groin, and they finally left.

I didn't know what to do. I didn't want to quit track, because I loved it and would have had to tell my mom. But then I didn't want to stay on the team because they might have thought I wanted more. I stayed on because I wasn't going to let anyone make me quit something I loved. After that, they never touched me again.

Michele--Age 16

In the summer between 7th and 8th grade, my family and I went to our cottage. I met a girl who lived up there year-round. We became friends, and she took me to places where the kids up there hung around. We went to the bike trails, and I met new people, mostly boys. One night we were invited to one guy's house. His parents were not home, so it was just five kids alone. We sat watching TV for a while until, one by one, the three other kids left. I got nervous, so I picked up a magazine. Rob sat next to me on the couch and took the magazine from my hands. He leaned toward me, put one hand on my leg, the other on the back of the couch. He started to kiss me on my lips and neck.

I pushed him away and said, "What are you doing? Cut it out!"

As I pushed him off again, he grabbed my wrists and

pinned me down. I was so scared I froze up, and he continued to slobber all over my mouth and neck. He was kissing me on my chest as far down as my shirt was unbuttoned. Then he let go of my wrist and helped himself to my shirt buttons. By the time I realized my hand was free, his hand was in my shirt and going for my bra. I swung my fist on the side of his head, and he sat up and called me a bitch. He came down on me again, and I lifted my leg quickly between his legs. He grabbed his groin and fell off the couch. I jumped up and ran out. My three other friends were waiting outside. They were shocked and angry at him when I told them what happened. I cried all the way home. Now when I see him, he glares at me like I was the wrong one. I don't know why he thought he could do that. I didn't even like him! After that, I've never let another guy do that to me.

Joan--Age 14

A couple of years ago in 8th grade, I hung around with three girls. Every day we would eat lunch in the cafeteria and then walk around the halls. Well, one day, as were walking down the hall, this guy Jason was coming towards us. When he got up to us, he grabbed my chest. I slammed the fries that he had in his hand into his face. He got really mad, and since he was not a small guy, I ran. I felt so humiliated and dirty. I kept thinking that my friends thought I was a slut. I cried almost every day when I got home. Ever since then, I get really angry whenever a guy starts grabbing at me.

Sue--Age 14

It was last summer when I went to the mall with my friend. We both went into a bookstore to look at magazines. This guy walked up and just started to talk to us. He was about 16. It didn't bother me at all, because he looked nice, and I thought he was just being friendly. I started to walk away with my friend. He followed us around in the store. That's when I started to worry. I told my friend that he was following us, and she told me I must be crazy. We ended up ditching him, but I still think back on that day, wondering if something would've happen to me or my friend. I was also frightened that something might happen to some other person who got caught in his trap. I've gone on and haven't worried about it much anymore, but once in a while it comes to mind. If it were to happen to me, I'll be prepared and won't take any stupidity from others.

Kim--Age 14

Before taking your class, I was afraid to go anywhere by myself, or be home or outside by myself. Just a few nights ago, it was late, and I was waiting outside the library for my mom to pick me up. I heard a rustling sound in the bushes and then a low laugh. Normally I would freak out and run, but I just backed up to the door and waited. I began to see this person coming out from the bushes, but right then, my mom drove up. I'm grateful for not being hurt in any way.

I feel I did well in your class because of my previous experiences. Dan, your calling me "Killer" helped me remember my past. It's a coincidence, but my classmates at my old grade school also called me "Killer." It started when this guy, really huge, started to beat up on me. I decked this kid so hard, he doubled over in pain, and then, just to make him learn his lesson, I kicked him right in the groin. I surprised myself because he must have come at least a foot off the ground.

Thanks for the extra boost of encouragement. Now I won't let those sick people stop me from carrying on with my life.

Grace--Age 14

Last summer I went out with this guy, and his father got a little close. I was working at a carnival with him and my boyfriend. Whenever he did something for me, he would say, "You owe me a kiss."

I thought he was kidding. Then at the end of the night, I went to his car (by myself, I thought) to get my things. He came up behind me and said, "You owe me kisses."

I just said, "Get away."

Then he grabbed me and tried to push me into the car. I

screamed and kicked because my brother who is a junior told me to do that when I was little.

Well, I ran away, but not before he ripped my shirt. To this day, I can't face either of them anymore. Before this class, I thought I did something to make him do it, but now I know it wasn't my fault.

Joelle--Age 16

I just recently had an experience of a sexual assault. I was at Bill's Pub after a basketball game, and this guy I sort of liked asked me to talk to him. We went over to the side, and he was telling me how much he liked me. Then I told him that I really liked him. He took that for granted, and started feeling me in places I didn't even know I had. He was really a large, muscular guy, and he held my arms. Then I thought of my choices in this kind of situation. I chose to use force.

I kneed him in the groin, and then my friend Keith came over and beat the you-know-what out of him.

I couldn't believe that he would do that to me. I'm so glad I had taken your class so I knew what to do.

Chris--Age 16

There was once a time when my boyfriend and I were at his house alone. We were sitting downstairs watching T.V. He got up to change the channel and came to sit by me, almost landing on me. He started to kiss me forcibly, but I slapped his face. He apologized, but he tried it again. This time he pinned me on the floor and sat on top of me, my arms under his legs. I screamed because he was trying to go up my shirt.

But no one was home except me, him, and the dog, who licked my face. As I lay there, I thought--what can I do? Then it occurred to me that my legs were free. I kneed him in the back, and he looked at me and went to grab my feet.

I got my feet and legs around his neck and pulled him down, which loosened his knees. I got up, grabbed my coat and purse, and left. I never saw or spoke to him again.

Maggie--Age 14

    The People Against Rape class was a big success for me. I learned that I am a special person, and I should be myself. There is this #1 jerk on our bus. He does things like picking his scab off with a razor blade and wiping the blood on the seat. He says some things to me and my friends that would make you want to throw up. We were talking about him once, and one of my friends told us that she felt "dirty" after he spoke to her. As it ended up, we all felt that way.

    But now that we've taken your class, we are no longer putting up with that. What he says to us is almost like a rape. He's taking away our pride and our self-respect. We definitely don't need this. If he ever says anything to us again, he'd better look out.

Tara--Age 14

    I really liked your class. Both of you are funny, energetic, and honest. I used to think rape was something that just happened to a girl. Once a man decided to rape her, that was it--she had no way to stop him. Now I know that's not true.

    About a year ago, my boyfriend wanted to have sex, and he made me feel like I had to--I owed it to him. He kept trying to talk me into it, and when I said no, he got really mad. Finally, he broke up with me because I kept turning him down.

    I was very upset. I felt like I should have had sex with him and was mad at myself for not doing so. My friends were really supportive and told me I made the right choice, but I still had doubts. He made me feel I wouldn't be worth anything unless I wasn't a virgin. Now I look back and know for sure I made the right choice by not having sex. Your class has helped me so much in dealing with that problem.

Michelle--Age 15

    I am so glad you came back this year. For the last few months, I have been feeling bummed out and sort of depressed. It just seemed like everything was going wrong. Most of my classes are very boring and do not help to brighten the days. Your class did help.

I've been feeling really good about myself the last week or so. I've started to demand some respect from people that don't usually give me any. Your talks about Positive Mental Attitude really helped. It wasn't that I never had a good attitude toward life, but sometimes I get in a slump and need to be reminded.

You have a great way of really reaching out and relating to teens. Somebody should make a movie about you guys. You're probably two of the best people I've ever met.

Good luck and thanks so much for everything.

Hope to see you again.

Sue--Age 15

Your class was thoroughly enjoyable, as well as educational. I have taken a karate class before, but the way you get people to respond and involve themselves is wonderful. You are two of the greatest teachers I have ever had. You have reinforced my confidence and belief in myself, and I feel better about fighting back for what I stand for.

I now understand why you are doing this. By educating our generation, you are turning out a whole new group of people who will hopefully help each other to help others. I think that's great, and I hope your mission succeeds. So far, it's fantastic.

Thank you for coming back this year. Please come next year — we'll all be waiting.

Andrea--Age 15

A couple of weeks ago, this guy Tony couldn't keep his hands off me. This happened after school when I was walking home. I was crossing the street, and Tony called me over, and of course, I went. We went out on a date once, but this day, he was stoned.

When I went over by him, he started coming close to me and hugging and kissing me. So I kneed him in the groin, but he did the same thing to me. I grabbed his groin really hard, and then he let go.

Marisal--Age 15

About a year ago, my mother was in her mobile classroom, teaching her first-grade class. She heard someone knocking and went to open the door. A guy came and shoved her into the bathroom. All the kids ran out to tell what happened.

The guy tried to rape my mom. She didn't let him, so he punched her in the eye.

Outside, a mother was coming to return a lost lunch box. When the guy heard the knock, he ran out the back way with my mother's chain. One of the little girls had already informed the principal and my mother's sister, who also works at the school.

They took her to the hospital and called my father. Then they went to the police. They never did find the guy. A few weeks before this happened, my mother had seen this guy looking around the school, so they think it was planned.

I felt I wanted revenge for that fool hurting my mom.

Kelly--Age 14

I went out to the show with this one stud I thought I knew really well. Everything was all right until he started moaning to himself and making strange noises. At first I thought I was hearing things, but it was him. He didn't say anything, but through the corner of my eye, I saw him playing with himself.

I freaked out! I didn't say anything, but got up, and walked away.

I still see this guy once in a while, but I completely ignore him. I didn't tell anybody about it. The picture wasn't dirty, so I figured it was just one of those days.

Violet--Age 15

One time I was at my best friend's house, and she went downstairs for something. Her dad started coming on to me, kissing me. I pushed him away and told him to stop. Finally I got so fed up I told my friend. He doesn't do this any more.

My same friend works at the church rectory, and the priest

comes on to her. She doesn't know what to do because she thinks no one will believe her.

Frances--Age 14

About a year ago, my sister was walking to work. She heard someone following her. She turned around and found a man holding a knife. He told her not to scream, but my sister was smart. She turned around and starting screaming and running in her heels. The guy threw himself on her, and she just kept on fighting. She knocked the knife out of the guy's hand and kept punching him. Finally he couldn't take anymore and got up and ran in the opposite direction. My sister ran, too.

We never found the guy who did it. We hope his next victims (if any) will fight and do as my sister did. I taught my sister the procedures, but I guess she should be teaching me something.

Kim--Age 15

A few years ago, I was visiting a really good friend of mine, and her father was staring at me. We were in the basement. Kelly, my friend, was sent upstairs by her father to set up the VCR. When we were alone, he started kissing me on the lips and saying he wasn't going to hurt me. By that time, I was shaking and crying, and Kelly came down. She knew what had happened. But she was mad at me. She went back upstairs, and he picked me up and kissed me. I spat in his face, and he put me down. I ran home.

I'm still friends with Kelly, but I never visit her.

Judy--Age 16

Just two days ago, I was at work. There is a guy I work with named Duke. He is 6'2" and must be pushing anywhere from 275 to 310 pounds. He is huge. I went into the back storeroom to get something. I got the feeling that someone was behind me. I turned around, and just as I did, the lights went off. Some light was coming in, and this made me able to see that it was Duke.

I freaked at first. I started yelling and screaming for him to turn the light back on. Finally he did. I tried to get out the door, but he blocked it. Then when I tried to kick him in the shin, he got mad. He pinned me against the wall and started pushing himself upon me. I got scared and angry, so with all my might, I kneed him hard right in the groin. He fell to the floor and threw up. I got away, but he hasn't been to work since. If it wasn't for what you taught me, something else could have happened.

Kelly--Age16

A couple of years ago, I was in the park near my house with this guy I really thought I liked. (As it turned out, he was a fool!) We were on the swings, and when I got up to leave, he followed. I thought he was going to walk me home, but I thought wrong. He pushed me down, and I quickly got up and told him that really wasn't very nice. The next time his hands began grabbing at me, I gave him a swift kick in the groin, and he said, "Okay, I was just joking."

Then I left. I don't talk to him, and he doesn't say much to me, but that's great in my book. I'd rather have it that way.

Beth--Age15

A few months ago, I went to this party, and a male acquaintance said he wanted to talk to me. He didn't do much talking, but his hands said a lot! He put his arm around me, and I took it off my shoulder several times. Then he placed it on my knee, and it was still wandering.

I didn't want to embarass the guy by saying something loud, so I just got up and went into another room with my friends. After this class, I realize that I should have embarassed him, so he would have gotten the picture sooner.

He did this the next few times I saw him, too, and he wouldn't have, if I had embarassed him by saying something so others could hear it.

Lisa--Age 15

A friend's father started to get too chummy. He started to put his arms around me and asked me to call him "Daddy." I refused, but I started to follow my friend around the house because I was afraid to be alone with him. I stopped going over to her house, because I didn't know what to do about her father.

A few weeks later, another friend of hers asked me if I had problems with the father. He had tried to rape her, and she felt it was her fault. Now I know it wasn't her or my fault.

I felt bad that I lost a friend because her father is a pig. I talked to her other friends, and now we invite her to our houses. I see now that by not going over to her house, we prevented something bad from happening to all of us, instead of just one.

Kelly--Age 16

I was jumped about one month before this class. Two guys, both of whom I considered to be my friends, carried me up to the bedroom and tried to take off my pants. Luckily, I have two brothers who have really taught me how to fight back.

They couldn't get my pants off because I wrapped one leg around the other and, for the life of me, I would not let go. I knew my life depended on my not giving in to them. I bit them as many times as I possibly could, and I cried--not to make them feel sorry for me, but because I was terrified! Finally their friend and my friend, too, came to my aid and helped me get away.

I saw one of the guys the other day, and as hard as I could, did the kick and recoil to the groin. Boy, was he in pain! The others in the "army" know, so maybe they'll learn some manners now.

Stacey--Age 16

My sister and I were walking through Lakehurst Shopping Mall when we came across one of her ex-boyfriends (whom she still had feelings for) and one of his friends, who offered us a ride home. My sister wanted to go, so I said, "Sure!"

They parked the van on the side of the street where I live

and tried to force us to have sex with them. I quickly grabbed the boy in the groin and twisted it, sticking my fingernails in. At the same time, my sister was doing some self-defense devices she learned in your class.

Soon the boy I was supposed to be with said, "Okay, I give up." He opened the side of the van.

My sister and I got out. While we were walking home, I said, "Thank God for Dan and Marie."

Amy--Age 15

Your class has really helped me a lot more than I expected. It brought my mother and me much closer. I never felt I could talk to my mother about sex or rape, because I thought she would say I was thinking dirty. Now I know how my mother feels about this, and I never expected such strong feelings about rape coming from her.

When I told her that rape is never the woman's fault, I figured she'd say, "Oh, now that's not true," in her motherly way.

But she agreed with me and said, "That's very true, and don't ever forget it."

She said if anything bad happens to me, or if I have a fight with a boyfriend, that I could always come to her. And now I know I will.

My mother has only one regret--that she couldn't take the class with me. But that's all right. Seeing as much as I learned, I told her I'll teach her all about it.

Lisa--Age 16

About two years ago when I was visiting my relatives during the summer, I met this guy. He was a friend of my cousin's boyfriend. He seemed really nice, and we all went out a few times. One time he asked me out alone, but he didn't say where we were going. He took me back to his house, and I soon found out no one else was home. He tried a lot of things on me, and I kept saying no, but he didn't stop. I was really scared, so I gave in until he wanted just too much. I kneed him in the groin really hard. He stopped, and I made him take me home. I felt guilty about hurting him until I took this class. Now I wish I had done it sooner and harder, but at least he got my point.

Michele--Age 15

Like last year in the Rape Seminar, this year you've done a terrific job. I think it was a great idea to have a co-ed class. I only wish my boyfriend could have taken it with me. One night we went out, and we started talking about your program. He's usually not a jerk, but this time he was teasing me about it and kept saying, "Let's see how you could defend yourself."

I said, "Do you really want to see how I could defend myself? Do you really?"

He said yes, and grabbed my shoulders tightly.

I made a quick grab for his groin and clamped. He let go, backed off, and squeaked, "O.K., you got me! I believe you! I believe you !"

He almost passed out. I proved that I wasn't going to take any garbage from anyone, not even a person I loved.

Your class has taught me a lot. I learned that my three natural defenses may be more of help to me because they may keep me from getting into a situation where I'll need the self-defense you taught to me. Hopefully, I'll never be in one of these situations, but if I am, I think I will be prepared to fight for my life.

I'm sure the whole class appreciated everything you've done for us. I think if any one of us is attacked, after finishing with our attacker, we should leave a card that says, "Compliments of Danny & Marie."

Dave--Age 16

About two years ago, when I was in 8th grade, we had a pool party at a girl's house. It was the end of the year, and we had no more school.

A few of the guys and I were in the pool with her, and we got an idea to try to get her suit off. Next thing you know, we jumped her--maybe about four of us. Now, at the time, we thought it was a big joke. We got her suit down a bit and started feeling her out. She kept resisting and saying no--which we interpreted as yes. You know, we said, "Oh, she loved it," and all that bull.

I had thought that it was no big deal, and we didn't do anything wrong. Besides, she and I are best friends now, and were back then after it happened, too. But after hearing what you said about it, I realized I was wrong, and I went up to her and apologized. We joke about it now.

Tammy--Age16

I am 16 years old now, but when I was 14, something very frightening happened to me. I had been seeing a guy who was a sophomore when I was a freshman. We would go out for walks and go places on a one-to-one basis. We were going together for three months. One Sunday afternoon, as my mom and I were walking home, we saw my boyfriend across the street. He asked me to go with him to a gym where we both worked. My mom said to go ahead, and she went on home.

As I got to the gym, I saw that only he and his best friend were there. They pulled me inside the gym and into one of the bathrooms. I had no idea what they were going to do, but I was very scared. My boyfriend held me down while his best friend tried to take off my pants and top. I was screaming, crying, kicking, and punching. Nothing I did could stop them. Finally, I broke free and ran. Once I got out of the bathroom, I saw my best friend in the gym. I felt a lot safer then.

I was fired because of what happened. The priest that I worked for said that it was my fault. After having talked with People Against Rape, I finally realized that it wasn't. The worst thing was that I really liked the guy, and all he said was that he was drunk at the time.

Thanks so much for all your help and support. I hope this letter can also help another girl see that if she got attacked, it wasn't her fault. Even after I got attacked, I wasn't afraid to go out with other guys. Girls have to go on and realize that not all guys are jerks.

Patti--Age 15

I really enjoyed your class. You have a certain way of relating to people that puts the listeners to ease. You really get your point across. I feel special now, and I'm ready to let others know that if they ever try to hurt my pride, or if they don't respect me, that I won't take it. I've really never been in a situation like the ones we discussed, and I hope I never will, but I feel that I can at least defend myself and handle the conflict more carefully. Now I feel that any problems (religion class grade, my sister, or my insecurity) can be overcome because, like you said, "We are special," and because we are special, no problem is too big to make us feel otherwise.

Carrie--Age 16

Your class has taught me so much. For one, it taught me that girls are special, and that we shouldn't put up with the crap guys give us. Please don't get me wrong, I know some very, very sweet guys, and they are great. But I have also had one too many experiences when guys have mistreated me. Now I don't take that from them.

I also feel more secure about myself. I think the self-defense makes me feel safe about being home alone or going out at night. I don't think I'm an animal or anything, but I feel that if I wanted to, I could hurt someone.

Most of all, you have made me feel good about myself. That I cannot explain, but last year and this year, too, you made me feel better about myself. All I can say is "thanks."

Kim--Age 14

This summer when I was at a party, everyone was drunk. My friend was lying down in a bedroom resting. Then two guys came in, locked the door, and started "playing" with her. I was in the next room, and I could hear her screaming and yelling, "Stop!" and "No!"

A friend and I started banging on the door. Their friends came to the door so no one would disturb them. They finally stopped and left her lying there. They had big smiles on their faces when they walked out. I went in the room and knew she had been crying. I asked her if she was okay, but since everyone was there, she said, "Yeah, it was nothing." I knew how she really felt.

Next day, people were talking about her and how she was an easy girl, and how she loved it. I got really upset because I knew the whole story, and she was a good friend of mine. If I told anyone the right story, they probably wouldn't believe me.

One of the guys told me to tell her that he was sorry. The other guys were older, and she is afraid to go near them.

I never realized exactly, at the time, that it was a form of rape. Taking your class has made me understand that if you say no, you mean it! And they should know it, too. Thanks for all your help.

Mary--Age16

Before your class, last year, I had my first and only experience, so far. I was riding in the bus, and this boy hopped in my seat. That was fine because I've been friends with him for four years. We were talking for a while, and all of a sudden, he started getting really perverted, pinching and poking at my chest.

I gave him a dirty look, called him an asshole, and punched his groin with my fist. I know the language wasn't necessary, but it was the first thing that popped into my head.

After I punched his groin, he left my seat in tears, practically, and the next day, he apologized. He never tried anything like that again and has been the sweetest guy to me ever since.

There have been a couple of times at school that we had speakers come in and talk to us about rape like we were babies. I got absolutely nothing out of it. I'm glad there are people like you to teach as you do. Your class is the most enjoyable and productive class I've ever taken. I wish every woman in the world could take it.

Chris--Age 16

I think that your class is great! I learned so much from you guys, both this year and last. You have made me feel better about myself. You also made me realize that not all guys are jerks.

Over the summer I went out with this guy who is two years older than I am. I really liked him from the start. We got very close. I thought I could trust him, so I told him a lot of things that no one else knows. We did everything together. He made me feel so good about myself.

After we had been going out for about three weeks, he was like a totally different person. He started pressuring me to have sex with him. He told me that he was a virgin, so it would be special for both of us. I thought he really liked me, but I also thought that he was using me. He told me that I owed it to him for all the things he had given me and all the time we had spent together. My brain must have been on vacation, because I believed him. After I did what he wanted, he dumped me.

After that, I was afraid to trust guys because I had really loved him. You made me realize that I didn't owe him anything, and that all guys are not like him. Knowing that has really changed me. Thanks a lot!

Patty--Age 17

I've already taken some of your advice and put it to use--Saturday night. My boyfriend is in boot camp for the Marines. Well, Saturday was our one-year anniversary, so I celebrated--and I do mean celebrated! Well, this one guy kept coming on to me and was being quite obnoxious. Now I was buzzed, but not drunk. He trapped me in this room where I was looking for my friend. He didn't like the words "no" or "get lost." He was getting real mad, and I was getting scared. He tried to kiss me, so I decked him in the face and then kicked him in the groin. He started running after me, and I was finally escorted safely out of the party. If it wasn't for you, I don't think I would have had that courage. So, THANK YOU!! God only knows what he could've done.

Krista--Age 16

Through your class I have learned how special each person, including myself, really is. Now I have enough courage to tell people what I really think and to tell them that I don't have to do anything that I don't want to.

For example, this one girl was always making me do things for her. I never said anything, because I felt I needed all the friends I could possibly get. Once, she asked me to hold her garbage from McDonald's until we got to a garbage can. I ended up just leaving it on the ground, but I didn't let her know that. Now I know that she was "using" me, and that I should have just told her that I'm not a garbage can. Too bad if she is no longer my friend. I know now that she is no friend of mine, and I'm glad! I guess I've learned to respect myself more and to do only the things I want to do.

Both of you presented things the way they are--realistically. The dating scene I felt really represented our whole society. I only wish that it would work like you said it should-- where two people tell each other that they like each other, and tell all their honest feelings in the beginning.

I really enjoyed this class and learned many things from it.

Sandy--Age 14

The other day, my younger brother Mike, who is 12, said that the self-defense techniques wouldn't work on him because he's too much of a macho dude, and he could "take me out" any day. For the last two years I've taken so much from him-- like being pushed and shoved for no reason. I never did anything in my defense because my mom said he was insecure about being the middle child. She knew I was fed up with him, though.

When he started pushing me, I was again letting him get away with it because my mom was there. He said, "See, I told you-- you're too much of a wimp to fight back with your silly self-defense."

So I looked at my mom and said to Mike, "You touch me one more time, and you'll regret it."

He laughed and tried to hit me. He just took a step, and I kneed him hard in his groin.

So far, he hasn't touched me since then. Thank you so much for the self-defense class. My brother will never bother me again.

Melanie--Age 14

There's this guy I've known ever since I can remember. He went out with my sisters, and he was a really good friend of the family. He and I became friends even though he's much older than I am (he's 21), and we'd go on walks a lot. One time when he put his arm around me, I mentioned the rape defense class, and he backed off. Then later he started coming on to me stronger, and I told him to cut it out or he'd be sorry, so he stopped again. But later it got worse. So I hit him in the face with all my strength and knocked him down and went home. After a couple of days he called to say he was sorry and asked if we could still be friends. We only talk on the phone now, and it seems he's really gotten to respect me. Your class helped me stand up for myself and not sit back and feel guilty later.

Jamie--Age 14

The thing that I really like is your firm belief in "It's never your fault!" Because even though this is true, some people like me need to be told. I also liked the way you stated "Life goes on," "What was in the past is in the past," and "Why live in the past when the present is here?"

I've found these all to be really helpful.

Kenya--Age 14

I have really enjoyed the class. It has changed me in more ways than one. You both have given me a new outlook on myself. I felt so down, and I was filled with hate towards myself. I have been through many different experiences in my life. Because of these things, I keep the way I feel bottled up inside of me. Some people can't remember far back. But I can remember as far back as when I was five years old. Sometimes I hate to remember my past because it scares me terribly. Almost every night I have terrible nightmares about things in my past. It confuses me so much because I don't know whether it happened or not. But your class has made me feel a little better about myself. I hope you will continue to teach. Good luck and thank you.

Lidia--Age 15

You have taught me a lot of things by what you have said in class and shown us to do. You really helped me feel a lot more confident and taught me that "Yeah, I am a special person!" I shouldn't let anyone have control over me, especially people I don't know or I'm not very close friends with. You have taught me not only to defend myself when someone tries to rape or hurt me, but also when someone like a so-called "friend" tries to control my life.

Now when I have to go to the alley at night to throw out the garbage, I'm not afraid any more because I know what to do.

I thank both of you very, very much! You came at the right time!

Shannon--Age 15

I'll be the first to admit that intimacy scares me right now. The last thing that I need or want at this point in my life is a serious relationship. Before I start sharing my life with anyone else, I've got to take care of me. So for now, I'm not planning on getting too involved with anyone.

While I'm at school, I want to enjoy dating, to keep my relationships platonic, and to date a number of men so that I can be exposed to all types. This way, when I'm ready to have a relationship, I'll know the type of man with whom I want to share the rest of my life.

I'm willing to admit I'm a virgin because I feel so strongly about it. Though I am sexually inexperienced, I'm also as aware as any other young adult of the power of body chemistry. I've felt that physical attraction. But I know that it doesn't always mean love, and love is what I want to wait for. For me, sex and love go together. So far, I haven't felt strongly enough about anyone to give him all of me.

I have learned that the first thing to remember is that you don't owe anyone anything. Always ask yourself what you want and what you think is best for you. Be honest about your own needs and desires. Don't let low self-esteem make you discount the importance of your feelings. If you feel uncomfortable about something that you're about to do, chances are good that you're not ready for it.

Any boyfriend who demands sex is not the right boyfriend for you. Don't let him trick you by making you feel guilty or weird because you're not willing to go along with him. If the situation gets out of control and you just can't cope, remember that you can always leave. He won't hate you. You'll probably gain his respect. Be firm about your decision.

Remember, Hands Off: I'm Special! Thanks so much, Dan and Marie. I love you both!

Chapter 11

Overcoming the Attack

We cannot stress enough the importance of getting counseling after you have been attacked. We don't mean counseling from your girlfriend, boyfriend, or parents. We mean professional counseling from a trained person. A rape crisis counselor, usually female, is your best bet. She is trained to understand your feelings in this situation. Many crisis counselors have been rape victims themselves, so they can relate to your experience on a personal level. Many of the rape victims to whom we speak are very comforted by the fact that Marie was a victim herself. They're not happy that it happened to Marie, of course, but they are encouraged that she has made it through the aftermath. They think to themselves, "Well, if she made it through that horrible experience, then I can make it. Things are going to be okay for me, too."

Do not stay with a counselor or psychiatrist who is not informed about rape. Many women claim that the psychiatrist blames them for the attack. Some are told to "forget everything," or "put your anger aside." None of this is good advice. How are you going to ever "forget" what happened to you? It would be abnormal to forget an experience that was so traumatic. We think it's okay to get angry. But make sure you get angry at the rapist, not at yourself!

It is essential to talk through your feelings. Allow yourself to cry. Suppressing emotions can harm you. Releasing emotions can help you. How can you get on with your life if you never get rid of the feelings that are bothering you?

Can you recall a time when you became angry with someone, and you didn't say anything to the person? The longer you avoided the discussion, the madder you got. Until you "got it off your chest," the anger just ate away at you. The same holds true for your emotions toward the attacker.

Find someone who will listen. Friends and family members will be more understanding of your feelings if you express them. You can't expect them to know exactly what you're going through, so explain to them in as many ways as you can.

The reporting and follow-up of the rape can cause you to endure more stress. Having to tell your story repeatedly, appear in court, deal with the red tape, and listen to the attacker's defense attorney are not easy tasks, but we believe you will actually become stronger from performing them.

Because we have found that getting involved in fitness had such a positive effect on our lives, we always recommend a fitness program to the women who want to do something to overcome the trauma of rape. Exercising is something that you are doing for yourself, not for anyone else. It will make you feel more confident and more capable of dealing with whatever life may hand you. It can be an excellent outlet for the pent-up energy from your many emotions. When you work out, you have to concentrate on the exercises and focus your attention on something other than your troubles.

Just remember, the feelings you are now experiencing will go away. You will not feel lousy forever. You will not be scared forever. You will not be angry and mad forever. The worst is behind you now. The worst is over. There is nothing you can do now to change what happened to you then.

If you would have known better, you would have done better. Tell yourself that all the time. This will put you at peace with yourself. By saying that over and over again, you will become the master of your own emotions, and you will not feel guilty for what happened. To quote a favorite author of ours:

"And how will I master my emotions so that every day is a happy day, and a productive one? I will learn the secrets of the ages: Weak is he who permits his thoughts to control his actions: strong is he who forces his actions to control his thoughts. Each day, when I awaken, I will follow this plan of battle before I am captured by the forces of sadness, self-pity, and failure.
If I feel depressed, I will sing.
If I feel sad, I will laugh.
If I feel ill, I will double my labor.
If I feel fear, I will plunge ahead.
If I feel inferior, I will wear new garments.
If I feel uncertain, I will raise my voice.
If I feel poverty, I will think of wealth to come.
If I feel incompetent, I will remember my past success.
If I feel insignificant, I will remember my goals.
Today, I will be the master of my emotions.

--Og Mandino
The Greatest Salesman in the World,

If you can follow the philosophy expressed in this poem, you can overcome not only rape, but any negative experiences in your life. Bad things happen to all of us. No one is immune from suffering and heartache. It's not what happens to us that makes us the people we are--it's how we handle those occurrences afterwards that really makes the difference.

"All right," you're saying to yourself, "this makes a lot of sense. I don't want to be an easy victim. I want to be able to defend myself. I want to develop my natural defenses. I want to be assertive and say no when I mean it. I want to get into good physical shape. I want to apply all the principles I've learned so far. . . but how do I do all this? I'm not used to expressing myself. I feel guilty if I speak my mind and hurt someone's feelings. What if I'm accused of being 'one of those feminists'? How do I become the person I want to be?"

To begin with, you have to understand that you are the most

important person in your life. That doesn't mean that you shouldn't care about other people, but you have to care about yourself first.

You have to rid yourself of guilt. Think of all the times guilt has kept you from achieving your goals. When you were planning to spend the evening studying for a test, your friends invited you to go somewhere with them. You told yourself it was the wrong thing to do, but you felt guilty about spoiling their fun, so you went along. You only got a "C" on the test, instead of the "A" you wanted. You were mad later for not having listened to yourself.

Now you have decided to learn self-defense and become a stronger, more assertive person. But people are putting you down for wanting to be that way.

"What do you want to be, some kind of guy or something?"

"You'll never do it. How could you ever defend yourself against a man?"

People will tell you what you can't do. When people tell you that you can't do something, what they mean is that they can't do it.

Tell yourself that you deserve more. "From today on, I'm not going to let others bring me down. I will walk away from negative people. If it is someone that I love, I will be strong and tell that person that I am going to be unaffected by negative comments."

Set a goal for what you want to achieve. Write it down. Be specific. Decide what it actually is that you want from yourself. Then concentrate on the steps necessary to achieve the goal. Don't let others sway you from your goal. It is your goal, not theirs. You can try to make them understand its importance to you, but if they won't, you have to stay on track anyway.

You must have a burning desire to attain this goal. If this is the case, you will give yourself wholly to it and be willing to sacrifice the time that is necessary. Remember, you deserve to spend time on yourself, not only on others. Be persistent. Don't give up. If you think you can't, you won't. If you think you are nothing, you will be nothing.

You might have to take some risks. Some people will not like the "new you." Some people can't handle other people's success.

These are not really the kind of people you want to have as friends, anyway. A real friend would share in your joy of accomplishment.

All of this ties into rape prevention in that if you are a strong, assertive, self-confident person, you will be more likely to fight back successfully if someone tries to force his will upon you. You would be less likely to be targeted for an attack in the first place.

If you have already been the victim of a sexual assault, you can still apply all of these principles. Understand that what happened to you is in the past. Accept the fact that you cannot change the past. Do not dwell on how bad your life is because you were raped. Say to yourself that you are not going to let the person who raped you control your life any more.

Do not hate yourself or allow yourself to feel guilty. You did nothing wrong! Remember, "If I would have known better, I would have done better." Get on with your life. Turn it around! A "positive" is only a "negative" turned inside out. Learn from your experiences, and change your future. You are going to prove to yourself that you can overcome anything, even something as horrible as rape.

We remind rape survivors that they are lucky to be alive. We ask them to get up in the morning and say to themselves, "I'm thankful I have one more chance today to change my life. I'm thankful I can see, hear, walk, talk, and breathe. I am thankful for a functioning brain. I am thankful for my natural instincts and natural abilities. I'm thankful I'm alive!"

Again we quote Og Mandino:*

> Today upon the bus I saw a lovely girl with golden hair,
> I envied her, she seemed so gay, I wished I were as fair,
> When suddenly she rose to leave I saw her hobble down the aisle,
> She had one leg and wore a crutch, and as she passed, a smile.
> Oh, God forgive me when I whine, I have two legs, the world is mine.

And then I stopped to buy some sweets, the boy who
 sold them had such charm,
I talked to him, he seemed so glad: If I were late t'would
 do no harm
And as I left he said to me, thank you, you've been so
 kind.
It's nice to talk to folks like you, you see, he said, I'm
 blind.
Oh, God forgive me when I whine, I have two eyes, the
 world is mine.
After walking down the street, I saw a child with eyes
 of blue:
He stopped and watched the others play, it seemed he
 knew not what to do.
I stopped a moment: when I said, why don't you join the
 others, dear?
He looked ahead without a word, and then I knew he
 could not hear.
Oh, God forgive me when I whine, I have two ears, the
 world is mine.

With legs to take me where I'd go.
   With eyes to see the sunset's glow,
With ears to hear what I would know,
   Oh, God forgive me when I whine,
I'm blessed indeed, the world is mine.

Dan and Marie's Daily Messages

The following statements reflect our philosophy on life.
We ask you to copy each statement down on a 3 x 5 card,
and carry one card with you every day,
repeating the message often.

1. I am nature's greatest miracle, and I am special.
2. Knowledge is power.
3. I am only a result of what I think.
4. Each day, I will be the master of my emotions.
5. There are no problems in life--only solutions.
6. If I am not part of the solution, I am part of the cause.
7. I will take action **NOW**.
8. I will persist until I succeed.
9. Today I begin a new life.
10. My life has a purpose--a reason for being.
11. What I believe, I'll receive. What I doubt, I'll do without.
12. To be truly happy, I must rid myself of all unnecessary guilt.
13. I'm not perfect, but I'm powerful.
14. I will keep on challenging myself until the day I die.
15. Success is a journey, not a destination.
16. I can see myself being the person I want to be.
17. I will always have the desire to better myself.
18. I will not settle for less.
19. The past is over--I will look to the future.
20. I will give up complaining and whining.
21. I am nature's greatest gift, so. . . **HANDS OFF!**